People with Autism Behaving Badly

People with Autism Behaving Badly

Helping People with ASD Move On from Behavioral and Emotional Challenges

John Clements

Jessica Kingsley Publishers
London and Philadelphia

The right of John Clements to be identified as author of this work has been asserted by him in accordance with the Copyright, Designs and Patents Act 1988.

First published in 2005
by Jessica Kingsley Publishers
116 Pentonville Road
London N1 9JB, UK
and
400 Market Street, Suite 400
Philadelphia, PA 19106, USA

www.jkp.com

Copyright © John Clements 2005

Library of Congress Cataloging in Publication Data

Clements, John, 1946 Dec. 1-
     People with autism behaving badly : helping people with ASD move on from behavioral and emotional challenges / John Clements.
     p. cm.
     Includes index.
     ISBN-13: 978-1-84310-765-1 (pbk.)
     ISBN-10: 1-84310-765-1 (pbk.)
     1. Autism. I. Title.
     RC553.A88C563 2005
     616.85'88206--dc22
                                                    2005001696

British Library Cataloguing in Publication Data
A CIP catalogue record for this book is available from the British Library

ISBN-13: 978 184310 765 1
ISBN-10: 184310 765 1

Printed and Bound in Great Britain by
Athenaeum Press, Gateshead, Tyne and Wear

Contents

List of Exercises

Note: Exercises marked with an asterix are repeated in Appendix 1.

Acknowledgments

I have worked with families whose sons and daughters have significant developmental disabilities for over 30 years now. It has been the most absorbing, stimulating and challenging part of my career. It is from the families that I have learned and continue to learn the most, both in terms of specific skills and general attitudes. I only hope that I have been able to give back something in return for what I have received.

Working with families throws into relief the core ingredients of behavioral work. Behavioral work requires that we stretch our brains to make sense of what is going on. It sometimes calls for courage when we are working around behaviors that are dangerous. It always calls for perseverance and determination because human behavior change is usually a slow, steady, unspectacular process. It calls for teamwork because we create better solutions when we work together. But there is one more ingredient that binds these others together – inspiration. We need a vision of what can be, a belief that we can achieve that and an energy to get there. So many families have provided that element to me over the years and they continue to do so. I wish that I could name them all individually but that would be a book in itself; and, I am sure, would also raise issues of confidentiality. Living in lawyerland one cannot help but be aware of such matters! I can thank specifically Paul Naleid for his insightful comments and help with Chapter 3.

I can also be more specific when it comes to some of the organizations and professional colleagues that are current sources of inspiration to me and enable even a grumpy old man to get it right sometimes. Parents Helping Parents in Santa Clara exemplify perfectly what families can do – the support parents can give to each other, the innovations they can stimulate and the vision that they can embody. I have been grateful for their support and encouragement over the last several years. My colleague Stephanie Lord, currently Principal at Heathermount Learning Centre (UK), has been a source of new ideas, new practice and positive vision for many, many years now. She continues to play that role and I am fortunate to have had the chance to work together with her for so long now. Bryan Craig and Erica Gould of The Centre for the Development of Autism Practice have not only done an excellent job in organizing my training work in the UK and in supporting and encouraging me but also exemplify in their own work that drive to 'make things better'. Finally Claudia Bolton and the team at Northstar Supported Living Service have shown me how a positive vision and an unerring commitment to individuals leading their own lives will enable us to work together to solve even the most complex and overwhelming of behavioral challenges.

Teamwork, commitment and inspiration – these are the things that drive technically sound plans to really make a difference in people's lives. Without these ingredients 'behavior guys' like me are reduced to the level of behavioral bean counters. I am truly grateful for the families and colleagues who have enabled me sometimes to get beyond the bean counting. I hope that this book will help others to do the things that can make a difference in people's lives but a book itself is of little value unless it is used by people working together energetically towards a positive vision.

Which seems to me very much what Jessica Kingsley Publishers is about. Their contribution to the lives of people with autism and their families is enormous. I am honored to be associated with that and grateful specifically for the help and encouragement that has been offered to me in the completion of this book.

To my family I can only apologize for inflicting on them once again the disruptions of writing another book. They have borne it stoically and not reminded me too often about the number of times I have said 'this really is the last one'.

Chapter 1

Read this Chapter

Thank you for taking the time to look at this book. Thank you even more if you have bought it! It is a book is written for the parents, brothers and sisters (adolescent and older) of children, adolescents and adults who have been identified as falling on the autistic spectrum. More specifically, it is written for the families whose autistic members are behaving badly and who want to do something to change that.

Behaving badly

Everybody behaves badly. Everybody does things that irritate, upset, stress or embarrass others. Behaving badly is part of the human condition. Families are especially good places for bad behavior. Family relationships are the most important relationships in our lives, the ties are the strongest and the stress level the greatest. We love each other a lot, we hate each other a lot, we do great things together and we drive each other nuts.

However, not all bad behavior has truly significant costs – it does not necessarily inflict significant harms. This book is about behaviors that *do* have very high costs – for the individual, for other family members, for the broader community. The costs themselves come in many different forms.

- *Physical costs* – the behavior may physically damage the individual or other people.

- *Social costs* – the behavior may make it hard to spend time with the individual or even to like him or her. The behavior may make it hard to visit with friends and relatives, hard to have friends and relatives over to visit, hard to find people to help out or work with the individual. The individual and family members are more isolated than we otherwise would be because of the behavior.

- *Lifestyle costs* – because of the behavior there may be places and activities that we would like to go to as a family but that we avoid. As a family we would like to go out to a restaurant, go on a vacation, go to a ball game, go to church; but the behavior makes that very difficult to do.

- *Financial costs* – we may have less money than we would have because of the behavior. It causes significant additional expenditures on items such as clothes, toys, equipment, furniture, carpeting or the structure of our house.

- *Emotional costs* – family members may feel exhausted, angry, hopeless and sad because of the behavior; and these feelings will not go away. They persist and affect many other areas of life (for example they cause conflicts in other family relationships – conflicts between parents or between the parents and the other children).

These are all significant, negative impacts and they fall on all members of the family.

The behaviors that create these costs are many and varied – various kinds of physical aggression, various kinds of self-injury, verbal abuse, rudeness, property damage, extreme and sustained noise, vomiting and regurgitation, smearing feces, insisting other people follow certain rules, refusing to accept direction.

Taking Cass anywhere in the car requires careful planning. He can become upset without obvious warning and will then start banging on the windows or will attack the driver. Windows in the car have been broken and on at least one occasion a serious road traffic accident was narrowly avoided.

Maria will not invite any friends over to her house. Her brother Alex tends to grab people hard and pull their hair, and for the last year has been refusing to wear clothes in the house.

Martha's mother has given up going out with all the kids together because it is impossible to predict whether Martha will get out of the car when they get to where they are going. With two other young children who are always keen to go, it becomes practically impossible to manage the situation if Martha refuses to leave the car.

The costs of a behavior relate to the type, frequency and intensity of the behavior. Some behaviors occur a lot of the time and that is what makes life difficult. Life would be more manageable if they only occurred every so often. Other behaviors occur rarely but are very severe when they do occur.

> Jack, aged 19, gets very angry but most of the time manages it well. However, about once a month he 'loses' it and when he does he punches, kicks and bites people with such ferocity that the police have sometimes been called.

The aim of this book is to give families practical ideas that will help to reduce the frequency and severity of costly behaviors. It offers no magic answers or quick fix solutions. It is about the little things that can be done in everyday life to make things better. It is about using the insights and skills that families have, and working away patiently in a spirit of optimism. We cannot magic away the behaviors that trouble us, but working together we can make a difference. We can help the individual to move on from resolving her issues in such costly ways and this will bring benefits to her, individual members of the family and the family as a whole. Exercise 1.1 (p.12) gets us started on the journey.

The exercise helps to get us focused on what we want to do and why we want to do it. It helps us to set priorities. This is a key skill – there are so many challenges in bringing up a child with autism that it is completely overwhelming unless we establish priorities. The exercise may even generate ideas about what needs to be done to make matters better. If so, you can put this book down and get on with life. But just in case the solution has not become obvious, we will next look in more detail at the content of the book and how you can use it!

Outline of the book

The book has four parts. Part 1, Groundwork, describes the starting points, the things to sort out before we get into detailed plans about how to alter everyday life to reduce problem behaviors. This includes pinpointing the behaviors to work on, screening for any underlying causes that might lead to a rapid resolution of our concerns and deciding on a consistent way of responding to the incidents that occur.

Exercise 1.1 Setting priorities, defining outcomes

List the behaviors of the family member with autism that concern you.

Put this list in order of priority, with the most important behavior first.

Take the most important behavior and identify the costs that the family is paying as a result of this behavior.

Write down what the individual should be doing instead of the bad behavior in the future – how will she deal with the situations involving bad behavior in the future if we get this right? What does she need to do to get it right?

Write down the differences that such a change would make to family life – what changes would there be in where you go, what you do, how you feel, who you see, what you or other family members look like (for example, in terms of bruises, scratches, marks)?

Part 2, Themes and Supports, gets into the specifics of behavioral work – the things that we can do to make things better based on our understanding of why the behavior occurs, what day-to-day needs it reflects. The part is organized in terms of common themes in behavior – what behaviors often tend to be about. Each chapter describes one of these themes and the kinds of work that will address the meaning of the behavior as we understand it. Several ways of working with a theme will be described (for example, there are activities to try, experiences to provide and skills to teach; ways to organize the environment, ways of communicating, ways of motivating).

Part 3, Underlying Issues, steps back a little from the specific themes involved in a behavior to look at two broader-based contributors that act as 'drivers' for some of the specific themes discussed in Part 2. These are loss of social engagement and loss of personal well-being in the individual with autism. It describes what these issues are and how they affect behavior, and offers specific suggestions for addressing the issues.

Part 4, Think Pieces, contains two short 'think pieces'. One, Chapter 13, reviews the use of psychotropic medications for behavior. The other, Chapter 14, discusses the potential contribution of developing an individualized 'relationship style' as well as the specific kinds of interventions that we usually consider when trying to effect changes in behavior. Although these chapters have important practical implications, there is less emphasis on 'things to do now' than in Parts 1, 2 and 3.

The final chapter, Chapter 15, considers how we view the needs of people with autism and stresses the very ordinariness of these needs. The challenge is in how to meet these needs, not in the needs themselves.

Using the book

Some readers will want to read the book cover to cover. Others will want to choose the parts that are most relevant to their particular family situation. I will now provide a guide to help those who want to 'dip' or who want to know in detail what the book covers.

Part 1 is relevant to everyone and should be read first. It is Parts 2 and 3 that have the greatest potential for 'dipping'. Each chapter addresses a specific theme that summarizes the cause(s) for behaviors and identifies specific ways of working to address the needs indicated by the theme. If you already have a sense of the key themes for the individual with autism in the family, then it is only necessary to read the relevant chapter(s) (a behavior may reflect more than one theme). To assist you in selecting which chapters are useful to you, these themes are now described in more detail. Part 2 begins with Chapter 4.

Chapter 4: I Can't Stand That

The theme of this chapter is behavior(s) of concern that are clearly triggered by stimuli that generate discomfort – the behavior occurs as a means of changing the situation or getting rid of the stimulus. Common triggers are noises (vacuum cleaners, lawn mowers, coughing, babies crying), words (specific words or phrases people use) or animals (especially dogs). The behaviors rarely occur unless these stimuli are present.

Chapter 5: You've Lost Me

This chapter deals with behavior that occurs mainly at transitions, waiting or unstructured time. Specific triggers include the autistic person:

- having to stop doing something that he is engaged in
- not knowing what is going to happen
- not having something to do, getting bored and doing something to relieve the boredom
- not having something to do and then doing something other people disapprove of which leads to a confrontation and a behavioral outburst.

As well as the specific needs, these kinds of situation can also lead the individual to being overwhelmed by external stimulation or internal stimulation such as anxiety. When he is in a structured or well-understood activity, or is helped to find something to do during waiting or other unstructured times, then the problem behavior rarely occurs.

Chapter 6: There's Something That I Want From You

In this chapter we examine those behaviors that are a means of persuading other people to change a situation so that it feels more comfortable from the autistic individual's point of view. The behavior may get the individual away from an uncomfortable environment, may get him left alone to get on with what he wants to do, may get him clearly noticed and focused on by others, may get him chased or held. The motivations are those that are generally important to the individual (individuals, of course, vary in their important motivations) – being alone, not being interrupted, being left to do what he wants to do, having high rates of (brief) social interaction, being chased or engaged in rough and tumble play. If the person is kept satisfied in terms of these basic needs, then the behavior is much less likely to occur.

Chapter 7: I Don't Want You To Say 'No'

The theme of this chapter is behavior that is very clearly triggered when the individual's wishes are denied. The behavior rarely occurs unless this happens. Sometimes the behavior may be effective in getting people to change their minds and give the individual what she wants. However, the behavior can still be triggered even if it does not change people's minds – the individual gets very upset, this escalates and she loses control when told 'No'.

Chapter 8: I Love It When...

Here we look at behaviors which are themselves a means for the individual to access known preferences in terms of sensory stimuli. The behavior is a way of indulging the individual's hobby or pastime. A person who loves oral stimulation may eat things that others regard as inedible. A person who loves squidgy textures may dig in his rectum and smear feces. A person who loves 'big messes' may rip things up and pour things out. A person who loves strong stimulation may throw furniture around or do things that make other people very angry. A person who loves dismantling things may destroy every household appliance. When the person is kept busy with other things or given ready access to approved ways of pursuing the hobby, the unacceptable behavior is minimized.

Chapter 9: I Feel Terrible

In this chapter we deal with behavior that is associated with a clear, temporary, negative mood state: when the individual is in a good mood the behavior is much less likely to occur. When she is in a negative mood there are likely to be specific triggers, such as those outlined above (noises, requests, denials), which precipitate the behavior; but behavior is not precipitated if these triggers occur when she is in a good mood. The mood impacts tolerance.

Chapter 10: I'm in Charge Here

The behavior discussed in this chapter occurs in the context of the individual taking up a position of power and laying down more and more rules for other people to follow (which words can be used; who sits where; who uses which rooms; who has access to the computer, the telephone, the television). If other family members do not follow the rules, then problem behavior (usually aggression) occurs as an 'enforcement' mechanism. As long as people do as they are told, the behavior does not usually occur. However, new rules keep getting added or old rules are changed so that it is very difficult for the family to accommodate the person in a way that avoids all aggressive outbursts.

Part 3: Underlying Issues

The specific chapters in Part 2 will identify when the broader themes discussed in Part 3 (Chapters 11 and 12) might be involved in the behavior. You will thus be prompted when reading Part 2, to dip into Part 3 in order to be most helpful to your family member. However, these are such important issues that I outline them here so that you get the chance to judge at the outset whether it is likely to be helpful to read these chapters.

Chapter 11: Loss of Social Connectedness

When you look at the broader context of the behavior, you will note some (more than one) of the features listed below. When you compare times when the behavior did not occur, or did not occur so often or intensely, with the present times when outbursts are occuring, you may notice that the individual:

- has very few social relationships other than with immediate family and people paid to teach or support the person in other ways
- rarely initiates social contact – rarely approaches others in any way for any purpose
- spends more time alone or away from others or engaged in activities that appear to be self-stimulatory
- is more focused on a particular topic which seems to generate a lot of discomfort and distress – this is often described as being more obsessional about something: more driven, but not in an enjoyable way. The issue seems to torment the person and be incapable of resolution
- is more resistant to direction
- is less tolerant of being denied things

- becomes distressed more often for reasons that are hard to understand and is harder to comfort and reassure.

Behaviors that are challenging are often more prominent when the person is less socially engaged. People lose their social engagement for a number of reasons, but once they are effectively isolated, withdrawn and lost within some kind of inner world, then this can itself become a significant contributor to the difficult behaviors. This means that rebuilding social engagement becomes part of the approach to effecting change in the behavior of concern.

Chapter 12: Loss of Personal Well-being

Behavioral issues become more prominent for some people in the context of a generalized loss of well-being. This is not just a passing mood, but a more pervasive state that lasts for days, weeks or months. Sometimes this is a recurring cycle that the individual goes through. When the person is in this state, problem behaviors occur more often and/or more intensely compared to the times when she is in a better frame of mind. When in this state some (more than one) of the following features will be noted.

Compared to previous times when the behavior did not occur, or did not occur so often or intensely, the individual:

- experiences an ongoing, diagnosable health problem (such as an ear infection or chronic constipation)

- appears to be in pain although no clear cause can be identified

- is more dominated by negative emotions (anger, anxiety, irritability) with positive emotions being displayed much less often

- is subject more often to explosive increases in emotionality – sudden outbursts – sometimes for reasons that can be understood, sometimes not

- cries sometimes for no obvious reason

- talks mostly about negative topics

- is more fussy and irritable in general

- sleeps worse

- has altered movement patterns (more active, more odd or apparently uncontrolled movements or, conversely, less active and getting increasingly stuck, sometimes frozen in the middle of doing something).

Restoring a sense of well-being then becomes part of the overall strategy for effecting a reduction in the behaviors of concern.

Part 4: Think Pieces

The chapters in Part 4 are more 'think pieces' than sources of practical ideas. The chapter on the use of drugs for behavior will only be relevant to those considering this step or who have general concerns about this issue. The chapter on relationship styles raises the possibility of being more generally effective with behavioral concerns so that reliance on highly detailed and specific behavior plans (which are notoriously hard to implement) can be reduced.

Exercise 1.2 offers a quick way for you to sort out which of the main practical chapters are likely to be relevant to the person with autism that you are trying to help. Chapters rated 3 or 4 are probably the ones to start with.

Concluding remarks

This book is written to be of practical use to families but it is also written in a spirit of partnership. It is about working together to resolve problems. The book contains lots of ideas, many of which have been 'borrowed' from the author's involvement with families over the last 30 or so years. The families who read this book will have a lot of ideas of their own. Thus the text should be seen as jointly owned and as a workbook rather than a shelf text. Each chapter will include space for writing down ideas that you want to try out or follow up on, whether these are ideas suggested by the book, new ideas that you develop as you read the book or things that you have found useful with the individual with autism in the past. Appendix 2 provides a 'learning log' so that you can track over time the things that you have tried, the things that worked and the things that did not work. It is important to be creative and to add ideas to the mix, not just to rely on the ideas described in the text. Above all it is important that you learn together with the individual whose behavior is cause for concern. Trying things, learning what works and does not work and remembering this allows the individual to 'speak' directly to you about his needs and your helpfulness, whether he has the use of words or not.

Exercise 1.2 Using this book – prioritizing chapters for relevance

Rate each chapter/theme in terms of its likely relevance to the specific behavior that you are concerned about.

KEY:

1	2	3	4
Does not apply at all	May apply	Applies some of the time	Applies a lot of the time

Chapter 4: I Can't Stand That

1	2	3	4

Chapter 5: You've Lost Me

1	2	3	4

Chapter 6: There's Something That I Want From You

1	2	3	4

Chapter 7: I Don't Want You to Say 'No'

1	2	3	4

Chapter 8: I Love It When…

1	2	3	4

Chapter 9: I Feel Terrible

1	2	3	4

Chapter 10: I'm in Charge Here

1	2	3	4

Chapter 11: Loss of Social Connectedness

1	2	3	4

Chapter 12: Loss of Personal Well-being

1	2	3	4

PART I

Groundwork

This section examines the first steps to take when we are looking to develop specific plans that will reduce a behavior that is causing concern. Chapter 2 looks at what behaviors to work on and the underlying causes that we should screen for before getting into specific 'behavioral' work at home. Chapter 3 works through how to decide on a consistent way of responding to the incidents that occur.

CHAPTER 2

What's the Problem?

Prioritizing

This is a book about behaviors that give cause for concern. Often there are several such behaviors. If so, it will be difficult to work on everything at once – that would be overwhelming for all of us. It is better to focus on a small number of concerns, make progress with those and then move on to other issues. Exercise 2.1 (p.24) helps to establish your priorities. It is an elaboration of Exercise 1.1, described in Chapter 1.

Behavioral work can take a lot of effort. It can be rather boring, but it is often effective. It requires problem-solving skills and then changes and adjustments in everyday life that we believe will make a difference. Everyone involved has to make changes. We ourselves have to make changes just as much as the person whose behavior concerns us; and no human-being likes to change. Resistance to change is not a specifically autistic thing. However, it does mean that often we try to change behavior just by changing the individual. This is unlikely to be very effective. Behavior is driven by interactions between the individual and the environment (the people, the activities, the physical qualities). Behavior change will therefore be about changes in both the individual and the environment.

Not only must we make changes but we must persist with them. Changes in behavior take time to develop and to consolidate. The results of our efforts,

Exercise 2.1 Setting the agenda

Write down each of the behaviors about which you are concerned. Be as specific as possible rather than lumping your concerns into more general categories like obsessions, resistiveness, tantrums. If it helps, imagine the person doing the things you are concerned about and write down what you see.

Behavior list

1.

2.

3.

4.

5.

Look at the list and think about the costs attached to each of the behaviors that you have listed (see Chapter 1 for a description of the various costs). Think also about the ones that bug or concern you the most (not always the most costly). Now write down the behaviors in order of priority – starting with the one that you would most like to see some progress on and working down.

Priority list

1.

2.

3.

4.

5.

Finally, write down the items that you are definitely going to work on – the ones that you are going to investigate further and make plans for. Choose no more than two items.

Commitment list

1.

2.

of the changes that we make, are often not immediately apparent. Only rarely are there spectacular changes. There continue to be good days and bad days but gradually, over time, we find that the problematic incidents are occurring less often, last for shorter times, are less severe…or all of the above. Sometimes a behavior of concern may disappear altogether, although this is the exception rather than the rule (for all human beings). It may be helpful to clear our minds of the wonderful graphs that are shown in journals – where behaviors occur a lot and then as a result of a magical intervention rapidly decrease to zero, never to occur again. It is more realistic to think in terms of our everyday knowledge of 'addictions' and how to change them – how to smoke less, drink less, exercise more, eat less, eat differently. This immediately makes it clear that change is difficult, that the course of change is uneven with frequent 'relapses', but also that change can happen and the benefits of the change are great. It also reminds us that there is a bit of a loss to change as well – letting go of old habits is a bit like losing old friends, even if those old friends were bad for us.

The reasons we do the things we do are murky and messy (rather than complex). Most behaviors are the result of the interactions of several factors, only some of which we will understand. Change often means working on several fronts. However, occasionally a behavior reflects a single clear cause that, if dealt with, may lead to more rapid, large-scale change. It is wise, therefore, to screen for certain things before getting into the detailed behavioral work described in this book, particularly (but not exclusively) if the behaviors of concern started rather suddenly.

Screening

The precipitants of more sudden behavior change tend to fall into four categories, described next.

Medical problems

Fortunately, research and practice since the early 1990s has paid a lot more attention to the kinds of medical problems that people with autism can suffer from. It has long been known that people with autism are vulnerable to a range of seizure disorders and that these can sometimes start later in life (particularly around adolescence). Not all seizure disorders are accompanied by a clear loss of consciousness; some will cause states of irritability and confusion and some can involve behaviors that look purposeful (suddenly running off, attacking others). It is therefore important to seek consultation with a neurologist if there is doubt as to whether the behaviors of concern might be part of seizure activity in the brain.

It has also become clear that people with autism are vulnerable to a range of gastrointestinal difficulties (chronic constipation, chronic loose stools, acid reflux, intolerance to gluten or casein, yeast infections). Controversy surrounds the causes of this association but it can certainly be the case that behavioral issues are much more prominent when gut discomfort is evident. Competent medical help with gut-related issues may then alleviate both the discomfort and the behaviors that accompany the discomfort. There is also some evidence that immune deficiencies and auto-immune disorders can be a vulnerability for some people with autism.

There are then the kinds of medical problems that can affect anyone but that are hard to detect for someone who has problems identifying and communicating about their internal states – headaches, sinus pain, allergies, ear infections, throat infections, joint pain. This also applies to more acute conditions such as appendicitis. There is even some intriguing evidence that on rare occasions mild streptococcal infections may be followed by the acute onset of 'mental health' problems like obsessive-compulsive behavior and that this can be alleviated by aggressive antibiotic treatment.

All this argues for considerable care before starting behavioral work and one should certainly not assume that all the behaviors commonly regarded as problematic are purely psychological matters, especially if there is a sudden change or repeated sudden changes in behavior. Basic medical screening and common sense medical treatments are important to consider first, if they have not already been considered. However, it is also important not to go to the other extreme – to assume that all behavior has a medical cause and that only biological interventions should be considered. This leads sometimes to a neverending pursuit of ever more implausible 'conditions' and the delaying of obvious common sense psychological work that would make a difference. As in all things balance and open mindedness are required and a close attention to the evidence, the things that we actually see. There needs to be more respect for careful observation rather than elaborate theorizing. Sadly, the field of autism is plagued by a lot of elaborate theorizing, often promoted by high status brilliant minds, and too little careful observation of individuals going about their everyday lives. As a parent, it is vital to trust what you have observed about your child and not the theories proposed by 'experts'. Use your own common sense and find medical practitioners who can share with you their common sense about the role of physical causes in behavior.

Trauma

Traumatic life events can have a major and dramatic impact on human emotional stability and behavioral functioning. Sometimes this effect can occur
after a single event (for example, a dog attack, a car accident) but more often
the effects are seen when there is repeated exposure to highly aversive experiences – repeated teasing and bullying, repeated harsh treatment (shouting,
hitting), repeated sexual abuse. It is a sad fact that people with autism are more
vulnerable than others to systematic abuse. This is a terrible reflection on the
people not identified as autistic who are supposed to be endowed with the
understanding of and empathy for others, the lack of which is portrayed as so
central to the difficulties for people with autism. Terrible it may be, but true it
is. If a significant change in behavior is noted it is important always to make
sure that traumatic experiences are not implicated. Removing these experiences will not usually lead to an instant 'recovery' but they do make possible
such a recovery, though the damage for some may be longlasting (not all
wounds heal completely – even with the best of help, scars can remain).

Changes in the physical environment

People with autism often have acute sensitivities to sensory inputs. They can
be troubled by sounds, colors, light patterns, physical arrangements of objects
in space. Thus, if the individual's customary environment changes and now
includes highly troublesome stimuli, then this may be reflected in his
behavior. For example:

- the opening of a kindergarten next to the school for a child
  troubled by children's noises
- a change in the road sweeping schedule so that now the road
  sweeper comes by during program hours rather than before the
  day program starts
- the repainting of a room
- a change to fluorescent lighting
- reorganization furniture layout
- moving to a workroom which has poor soundproofing so that
  noise from adjacent workrooms can clearly be heard.

These kinds of changes may not be reversible in which case your work has to
focus on building tolerance (see Chapter 4). But if there is the option of

reversing the change or making some other accommodation to the individual's sensitivities, this will be a much quicker solution than building tolerance.

Changes in the social environment

A stereotyped view of people with autism would suggest that relationships are not that important to them and that when friends or relatives leave their social circle it has little impact. Nothing could be further from the truth. Relationships are very important for people with autism and loss can be just as disturbing. What does differ is that quite often the response to loss is delayed – it may take some time for the individual for autism to register that something in his life has changed. It is not at all uncommon for someone with autism to give no immediate response to loss, even a grievous loss such as the death of a parent, but to suffer a very significant period of emotional behavioral turmoil six months later. Unlike the other factors described above there is no immediate 'fix' for social losses. It is important to build ways of documenting those who are a significant part of the person's life (for example, using photo albums). It is important to provide sympathetic support, reassurance and relief during the period of turmoil. However, if a significant behavior emerges at this time and is not reducing within a few months, then more specific behavioral work will become appropriate.

Follow-through from prioritizing and screening

Thus, having identified the behaviors that are giving rise to the most concern, the next step is to screen out potential causes that need to be dealt with by interventions that are not strictly behavioral (medical treatment, trauma relief, physical environmental alteration, social support). Such screening will usually involve approaching others (doctors and agency personnel) and seeking their input, which may involve some change in what they are already doing. Our contacts with these professionals will be relatively brief and those we approach may not always know us or the individual with autism very well. It is therefore important to present them with both our concerns and the observations that give rise to our concerns. Some ways of doing this are explored in Chapter 13 and Appendix 3.

The screening and the interventions that follow may deal with the behavioral issues completely (the behaviors may cease); more likely, they will lead to some reduction in the problem behaviors and there will be a need for additional behavioral work (because most human behaviors reflect the operation of multiple contributors not single causes). And, of course, in many cases there may be none of these factors involved, or, if they are involved, dealing with them fails to impact the behaviour of concern – the issues are more 'purely' behavioral. So, in most cases, once the work has been done to screen for and deal with these contributing factors, there will still be a need for behavioral work.

The usual way of presenting behavioral approaches is to turn next to assessment and detail how to assess a behavior so that we can understand it better. From the assessment we learn the best ways of improving matters (usually involving prevention and teaching some alternative skills). Assessment often involves charts and other forms of record keeping and tends to go on for some time (often several weeks). Intervention tends to focus then on prevention and skill-building but would include, at this stage, ways of responding to incidents so that the behavior is not reinforced.

This model presents a number of difficulties from a family point of view, particularly when the family is working alone, without access to competent behavioral support services. One difficulty is that families find charts and record keeping difficult – such activities do not fit easily into the rhythms of ordinary family life and often seem rather uninformative from the family's point of view. Another is that families can sometimes feel that they do not learn a lot from charts and records – after all, they already know their son and daughter pretty well. Such forms may help 'outsiders' who do not know the child well, but that is a different issue. The third difficulty of the 'assess first' model is that it does not address the first question that many families have: 'what do I do when she…?' Families are very keen to know how best to react to behavior. If professionals say, in effect, that they will get to that in a few months time, it can be a way of undermining the family's agenda and of implying that the professionals know best. Confidence is an important issue in behavioral work and anything that undermines a family's confidence will be counterproductive.

It is true that assessment can sometimes illuminate issues that are not already known and sometimes a focus on reacting to incidents slows up work that will deal with the issue more effectively in the long term. But assessment is not always illuminative and long-term work can sometimes only be considered once the family feels confident and secure in how it manages incidents. Thus the present book will not follow the usual sequence but will instead go on to consider in the next chapter how to respond to incidents. Although the meaning of behavior plays a central role in this book there will be no detailed consideration of assessment as there is a companion volume devoted entirely to this topic (Clements 2002).

Chapter 3

Responding to Incidents

The issues

When families are faced with significant behavioral issues they obviously want to know how to reduce or get rid of these behaviors. But they also have to deal with them day-in and day-out. So it is not surprising that one of the first questions that families ask is: 'What am I supposed to do when he...?' The smart answer is that how we respond depends upon what function we believe that the behavior serves. If the behavior is a means of avoiding doing tasks that are disliked, then we need to see our demands through; if it is a means of gaining stimulation then we need to reduce/eliminate the stimulation achieved; if it is a means of getting us to take notice then we need to make no social response.

However, the question of what to do about incidents can come up before we have a clear understanding about what a behavior means. Families are keen to 'do the right thing' but are not sure what the right thing *is*. They often receive conflicting advice about what to do. The net effect is to undermine their confidence in handling incidents. This lack of confidence, this uncertainty, readily communicates itself to the individual whose behavior is cause for concern. This can escalate her emotions and in turn both create more incidents and increase the severity or duration of incidents. The uncertainty may also mean inconsistency in the family's response, which can have a number of effects. It can make the person with autism more anxious, as predictability and ritual are important ways of making the world safe. It can mean that the problematic behavior is sometimes rewarded and sometimes not and this 'gambling effect' can make the behavior much harder to change. The inconsistency can also make it harder to interpret some assessment information – which of the several responses to behavior that appear on incident records might be the maintaining consequence (reinforcer), if there is such a thing (not all behaviors are functional)?

It therefore seems appropriate to try to stabilize our response to incidents as a very early step in behavioral work. Before we can make such a decision we do need to get clear what we hope to achieve by having a planned response. There can be a number of reasons for having such a response, a number of outcomes that we want to achieve. These include:

- to effect safety

- to teach the individual with autism about how the world is going to work from now on, what leads to what – what consequences the behavior leads to

- to teach the individual what she should be doing in the situation

- to teach the individual about how other people are impacted by the behavior

- to teach the individual about how other people will view her

- to teach the person 'a lesson'.

There are interventions that can be used to achieve each of these goals and it is of course possible to combine interventions to achieve a range of outcomes. However, if a behavior is dangerous, if the person or others are likely to be hurt as a result of the behavior, then finding ways to reduce the likelihood of harm has clear priority. This creates a dilemma for me. Many families will be dealing with behaviors that are very difficult but that do not carry a significant risk of substantial harm to the individual or others. If we start this chapter by detailing the very tough options faced by families whose sons or daughters do dangerous things this may be off-putting and discouraging for those readers not faced with these dilemmas. If, however, we fail to address safety issues and pretend that with the right preventative programs all safety issues will vanish then, as so often happens, those families facing these issues will feel marginalized.

The chapter will therefore start by considering ways of responding that are about effecting change, as this is relevant to everyone. The section on maintaining safety will be at the end of the chapter so that readers can easily skip that if it does not seem relevant to them.

Interventions for effecting change

Change is considered at two levels.

1. *The behavioral level* – we respond in ways that might directly influence behavior leading to change in that behavior in a relatively short time span (perhaps in terms of weeks or a few months).

2. *The cognitive level* – we respond in ways that seek to impact the individual's understanding and thinking so that over time he becomes more able to inhibit impulses to act, becomes more self-controlled. Here, the timeframe for change is months and years.

In order to present this in more practical terms, we will look at responding to behavior in terms of the 'messages' that we are trying to convey to the individual, the specific outcomes that we are trying to achieve by our intervention.

To teach something about how the world is going to work from now on, what leads to what – what consequences the behavior leads to

Many (not all) of the behaviors that concern us are functional in the sense that they achieve an outcome which is reinforcing for the individual. He finds that he does not have to do tasks if he head butts the people who are suggesting he does. Another individual, who feels lost, bored or anxious, now has comfort from someone because he started hitting himself. There is nothing like the joy experienced by hurling crockery to the floor and seeing and hearing it shatter into a thousand pieces. If we look at the behaviors that concern us from the individual's perspective, we realize that they believe that this is clearly how the world works so it makes sense to keep on doing the things that work well. If we want these kinds of behaviors to change then we need to change how the world works and make sure that these behaviors no longer achieve reinforcing outcomes – we need to:

- see through any instructions we give and not back off when the person head-butts us

- make absolutely no response when the person is hitting himself

- make sure all the crockery available is plastic/melamine so that even if it is thrown, it will not break.

To effect this kind of relearning requires great consistency (we must *never* allow the reinforcing outcome to occur) and great perseverance (the behavior will initially get worse and will only gradually improve). However, if we get it right, change does occur in the relatively short term. The learning is strictly behavioral, no cognitive change occurs and the behavior will quickly resume if we slip-up and reinforcing outcomes occur. The change will be longer lasting if we combine this approach with the others outlined in this book.

To teach the individual what she should be doing in the situation

This is about giving positive directions to the individual about what she should be doing now – prompting with words, gestures, signs, pictures or physical guidance the kinds of behaviors that would be regarded as acceptable in the situation (for example, taking time in her room rather than breaking up the living room, stamping on the floor rather than hitting her head, using words to ask for help rather than shouting and screaming). The incident becomes a teaching moment.

To teach something about how other people are impacted by the behavior

Here we construct a response that seeks to convey to the individual the social consequences of his behavior. We try to build his understanding of why he should not behave like this so that he can learn to inhibit the impulse to behave badly. Such a response may be a verbal explanation ('When you do that it hurts me'), a gestural explanation (pantomiming hurt, exaggerating the response), a pictorial explanation (a picture sequence showing that 'if' the behavior occurs 'then' the other person feels something or money has to be spent). The explanation should also include information about good choices to make in the situation, the alternatives that we regard as competent ways of dealing with the problem and how others will feel if good choices are made.

Such explanatory responses are fairly natural. Ingenuity is required in how you convey the information effectively to someone with autism. These responses are not likely to have any immediate impact on the likelihood of the behavior occurring again. They may contribute in the longer term to the slow growth of social understanding and this will enable the person in the long run to be more competent in managing his needs. There is no direct research on this issue although research in normal development strongly supports the value of explanations and research in autism clearly demonstrates growth in 'theory of mind' capabilities over time.

To teach the individual about how other people will view her

This is another more 'cognitive' intervention but one that emphasizes links between the behavior, how other people will think about you and how you like to think about yourself. It also emphasizes the fact that behavior can be controlled and is about choice. In our present state of competence it applies more to those people who can communicate with us verbally. It requires listening out for words that are important to the individual or directly questioning her using word lists and asking if this is a word that she wants said about her or not. It then becomes possible to attach behavior choices to the preferred/non-preferred words – acting out is being 'like a child', 'inappropriate', 'weak', 'bullying'; acting competently is being 'adult', 'appropriate', 'strong', 'nice'. This approach can be enhanced by lists showing the behaviors that attach to the key concepts and emphasizing the choices that can be made, and that the individual can choose to act like a child or an adult, for example. The response to incidents involves labeling the behavior in non-preferred terms and suggesting another behavioral choice that would have merited a preferred label.

> Lauren's grandmother is very politically incorrect. She says to Lauren, when she is starting to tantrum and injure herself, that she is letting her autism take over and needs to take control. Lauren has picked up on this and it seems to motivate her to control herself. We are developing this to try to frame choices between 'autistic' behavior choices and the choices that 'smart girls' make when they are upset. (We, of course, are fully aware of the broader issue about portraying autism as something negative, but the approach described here depends on working within the individual's cognitive frame of reference to convey important social messages.)

This approach is not a quick fix. On the other hand it is not as long-term as giving explanations, because it is based on concepts that the individual already has and uses.

To teach the person 'a lesson'

This is another more directly behavioral intervention that aims to decrease the behavior by levying a cost consequence. Cost consequences come in many forms. There are social costs – we make ourselves unavailable to the individual or send him away from us for a time. There are effort costs – as a result of the behavior the individual has to make some effort doing something that he would prefer not to do (tidying up the mess made, doing extra chores or work of other kinds). There are material costs – missing out on something that the person would have liked to do (for example an outing, ice cream) or having to pay/forfeit money. There are physical costs – inflicting some kind of pain (forbidden in most professional settings and in some societies altogether).

For costs to be effective a number of criteria need to be met. The individual must be generally sensitive to cost consequences (there are individual differences in this respect). There must be a significant cost to which the individual is sensitive that is available to us and that we are permitted to use. We must be able to levy this cost *immediately* following a behavioral incident. We must be able to levy this cost *every time* the incident occurs.

Aside from the ideological issues about the use of punishment or aversive consequences for individuals we regard as disabled, it is very difficult in practice to meet these criteria. Hence, in most circumstances, cost consequences are not a relevant intervention. However, they are a very natural intervention, a prominent part of parenting in many cultures, and can work with some individuals whom we identify as autistic.

How to decide

When it comes to deciding on how we should respond to behavioral incidents so that we effect change, we should think about the 'messages' that we want to convey. We may want to get over more than one 'message'.

> You hurt me and it's going to cost you.

> You're making a two-year-old's choice, but you are still going to have to get dressed.

If we are clear about the message then we can work out in detail how that message will be conveyed – what words, gestures, signs, pictures we will use, what tone of voice and body language we will use, what other elements will be part of our response. That is, we develop a script for the response and we follow that script each time an incident occurs.

Interventions for keeping safe

Prioritizing safety can force us to make tough decisions.

> I may know that you are banging your head on the concrete in order to get me to come over and hold you. From a strictly behavioral point of view I should ignore you. However, the risk of harm is such that I am not going to do that. I am going to intervene because that is the only way I can reduce the likelihood of you harming yourself.

I know that you are punching and kicking me because you do not
want to do the task that I have asked you to do. From a strictly behavioral point of view I should stay with you and see the demand
through. However, the risk of harm to me is such that I am not going
to do that. I am going to withdraw because that is the best way of
reducing the likelihood of harm to me.

I love you dearly. I know that you do not really mean to hurt me. I
need to be here for you to see you through these difficult times.
Therefore when you begin attacking me I will call the police for
assistance because otherwise you may hurt me so badly that I will no
longer be able to have you around, and that would be worse than you
being removed for a few days to a crisis center.

These are not decisions to be taken lightly. But if a behavior is clearly dangerous then our response must be driven by safety considerations. However, there
is no one right approach that we *must* follow. As in all things there are options
and choices. The choice will be determined by the nature of the behavior and
the resources available. One important consideration is whether there is a clear
build-up towards incidents, signs of increasing disturbance and escalation, or
whether incidents occur very fast without any warning signs that we are able
to detect. If there is a detectable escalation sequence then there are a number
of interventions that can diffuse this build-up and avoid incidents (clearly a
desirable outcome from most points of view).

Responding to escalation
Effective tactics include the following.

- *Reflection* – whether the person is verbal or not, is thought to
  understand or not, it remains important to acknowledge that she
  is getting upset and to express concern about that. This may be
  done in words and body language. This can both help to calm her
  directly and also inhibits us from getting into 'confrontational'
  mode. Being confrontational during escalation is more likely to
  accelerate the process than to diffuse it, although it can be an
  option to consider (see below).

- *Problem solving* – people get upset for a reason. It is obviously
  important to try to find out the reason and see if something can
  be done to address the concern. One of the difficulties that we
  face when supporting people with autism is that often the

communication gulf between us makes it very difficult to find out what the problem is. Hence our need to rely on the other tactics described here. However, these obvious difficulties should never lead us to assume that there is not a reasonable concern driving the person's increasing agitation.

- *Distraction* – here we are trying to shift the person's attention to another 'topic' by, for example, getting out an activity, drawing attention to something else in the environment, doing something silly or outrageous.

- *Calming* – we can do things that more directly bring down the level of arousal – putting on some calming music, massaging hands, feet or back, turning down the lights, reducing the noise level, perfuming the environment with a relaxing aroma, going for a brisk walk, eating a snack, moving the person to a low stimulation area.

- *Positive redirection* – we may clearly direct the person (with word, signs, gestures, pictures) to do something other than what he is doing right now. The redirection is likely to be to a distracting or calming activity. We must be more assertive and intrusive in order to help the individual focus and engage with the activity, which he might not do if we took a more passive approach.

- *Authoritarian control* – this goes beyond positive redirection and involves 'strong' and controlling body language, gestures and voice tone that communicate in no uncertain terms that what is going on will not be tolerated and that the person had better get on with something else. It uses a level of intimidation within which to deliver a positive redirection.

These approaches are not mutually exclusive and not all of them work for every individual. Some are high risk. For example, authoritarian control will escalate the situation for quite a lot of people. The approaches are likely to be combined into a sequence to follow, so that if one does not work or the person is escalating further, you move on to the next one (see below for how to plan these kinds of sequences). In many cases diffusion will be effective. But not in all. There are plenty behaviors which do not involve a period of emotional escalation or where the escalation is not detected by us. However good our preventive efforts, we still need to consider the response we should make once an incident occurs.

Responding to behavior

Once incidents are under way there are a number of possible options.

- *Do nothing* – one option is to do absolutely nothing and to allow events to run their course without any active intervention.

- *Clear the area* – move away from the person, move others away and let him calm in his own time.

- *Move the person* – physically move the person to a safe area and then let her calm in her own time.

- *Call for advisory support* – there may be access to an on-call support service that can work with you in terms of providing emotional support and guidance on the management of the incident in progress.

- *Call for physical support* – there may be access to other people at home or a specialist crisis support service that can send people out to help. Alternatively you may call the police for assistance.

- *Stay with the person: 'block' / 'break'* – this involves remaining present and using blocking tactics to maintain safety (for example, parrying blows with your hands or using a cushion to block blows either to yourself or self-injurious blows). This would also include breaking grips (for example, breaking away from bites, grabs to the body or hair).

- *Stay with the person: hold* – this would involve either holding a specific limb or more generally restraining the individual's body until he calmed down.

How to decide

The approach to managing an incident so that the likelihood of a safe outcome is achieved needs to be individualized. There is no standardized approach that works for everyone. The first step is to identify what we know already about specific supports that help to keep the person and others safe – things that diffuse escalation and things that help when 'the fists are flying'. Exercise 3.1 helps with this.

Exercise 3.1 Supports that help – what we already know

List what you know about supports – ways of working that are effective and ineffective with the person that you know.

	Supports that are generally effective/helpful	Supports that are generally ineffective/counterproductive
Ways of diffusing escalation		
Ways of responding to dangerous behavior		

The second step is to rule out those interventions for which there are no resources. There may be no-one else at home and no on-call advisory or crisis response service. There may be no other places to move others or the person to.

The third step is to evaluate the remaining options from a risk benefit point of view. For example, we stay with the person and block what are the likely benefits and what are the likely risks, knowing this person and how she reacts to things. From this evaluation will come an idea of which interventions are most likely to achieve a safe outcome. Safety cannot be guaranteed. We can only use our best judgment to reduce risk as much as possible.

If we have worked through this decision, following the above steps, and it is apparent that we will need to use any directly controlling physical interventions such as breaking grips, moving the person physically or holding in any way, then we are most certainly advised to seek out some training on crisis management, including physical interventions. Fortunately, there is now available a number of training packages that teach simple techniques for physical management in the context of respectful and caring relationships and without the punitive component that used to be the hallmark of 'control and restraint'. They also pay close attention to diffusion and prevention. These training packages are often freely available to professional staff who support individuals who do dangerous things; but there has been a slowness to recognize that many families are struggling at home to keep themselves and their children safe. The evidence is clear. An appropriate training package boosts confidence, reduces the frequency of incidents and reduces the likelihood of injury from incidents that do occur. If, therefore, it looks as though some kind of controlling physical intervention would help family members stay safe, then it is important to press local service-providing agencies to enable families to access the training opportunities that are most certainly going on locally or to create a training opportunity like this specifically for local families (in any local area there will be plenty of families facing these very painful decisions).

If our consideration of safety management brings us to the conclusion that we may on occasion need to call the police then it would be wise to make contact with the local police department to get some sense of how they view these calls and what, if anything, they know about autism. Although there is often considerable fear about calling the police (and not a little stereotyping of how the police respond in these circumstances), the police can be very good at responding and bringing calm to a situation in skilled ways, without the use of excessive force. There is also more attention now being paid to teaching emergency personnel about autism, so that it is becoming more likely that officers will bring some specific knowledge to the situation as well as their general competence at dealing with people who are out of control.

One of the problems in these discussions is that some of the options are very painful to contemplate, particularly restraining someone or calling the police. Because they are painful we would rather not consider them and therefore come up with strategies that avoid mention of them. That is fine provided that the strategies we come up with are effective in maintaining safety. The worst possible outcome is that we fix on ineffective strategies and then find ourselves having to use extreme interventions 'on the spot', without any planning or training. That is when things go seriously wrong and unplanned restraint leads to injury or a call to the police results in some traumatic experience for the individual with autism. It is important, therefore, to be realistic and to look at all the options before deciding on those that best fit our knowledge of the individual and the resources that we have available.

Having weighed up the options and decided those that seem most likely to keep everyone safe, these can then be put into a simple plan format. A useful format for doing this is to link specific behaviors of the individual to specific responses that we make – 'When s/he does... We will...' Below follow three examples of these kinds of plans.

When Tony...	We will...
Paces rapidly in the living room, jumping hard and squealing	Offer him a toy from his hobby box or put on a favorite video
Continues to pace, jump and squeal	Direct him to sit on the bean bag and offer an arm massage
Grabs or pushes at us	Look hard at him, speaking firmly with clear gestures: 'Put your hands down and move away' and we will physically guide his hands down and point to where we want him to go. We continue with this until he moves away and then we will encourage him again to sit down and offer an arm massage

When Frank...	*We will...*
Stamps on the ground and bangs on his chest	Ask him to tell us what the problem is. If he says nothing we will ask him if he hurts. If he says he hurts or we judge him to be in pain we will offer him the analgesic as per his doctor's instructions
Continues stamping and banging	Withdraw and give him his space. Check in every few minutes to see if he is OK or needs things from us, but otherwise not intervene
Comes towards us and starts swinging punches	Tell Frank firmly 'That's not OK', move round behind him, grab the waistband of his pants in one hand, put the flat of your other hand in his back and move him away, saying 'You need to take time for yourself right now'. Repeat as necessary
Continues to attack and we feel unable to keep safe	Withdraw to our bedroom and call the…service for advice on the next steps

When Katrina...	*We will...*
Wails and cries and throws things around	Remind her she is acting like a little girl and encourage her to make an adult choice and tell us what the problem is
Continues wailing and crying and throwing things around	Set up distracter activities (put some music on, get out the puzzles, start doing the washing up) and either busy ourselves with these or busy ourselves with something else (reading, writing notes). We will not respond directly to Katrina

Starts to throw solid objects at us or hit and kick us	Step right in close to Katrina and say very firmly with a serious expression, looking directly at her: 'It is not OK for you to hurt me, I do not accept that' and hold our ground. If she looks down and/or moves away we will move away and return to what we were doing
Is continuing to aggress with escalating intensity	Withdraw to our room, lock the door and call…for advice about continued management of the situation
Continues the aggression or property damage so that there is a clear threat to our or Katrina's safety	Call the police

Not all of the behaviors that cause concern are dangerous. And, of course, if we can build things that might help change the behavior or the person's understanding into a management plan then that is all to the good. But it is important not to lose focus on what we are trying to achieve by having a plan – the aim is to respond in ways that minimize the likelihood of anyone being significantly hurt. The key outcome is that people stay safe. We will have other plans for helping the individual move on from the behavior as a way of dealing with his issues, but when it comes to incidents, our guide is to ensure safety.

Concluding remarks

Developing a response to incidents means being clear about what we want to achieve and then working out the details of how we achieve that given what we know about the person, ourselves and the situation. Going through this process builds confidence and leads to greater consistency in how behavior is responded to so that overall a greater sense of stability is achieved for everyone. With this kind of stable platform it becomes easier to develop and implement plans that are focused more comprehensively on change. That is what most of the rest of the book is about – how our understanding of behavior leads us to effective interventions for change.

Although we have stressed consistency in responding, it is important to understand this as an aspiration rather than a routine real-world occurrence. All of us have bad days, days when we are stressed, we forget the plan or react impulsively in line with how we feel at the time. It is important not to feel disheartened about lapses – no-one is 100 per cent consistent, except in the most artificial of circumstances (which is why behavioral interventions often have limited real-world viability). That is why we have emphasized here the importance of clarity of purpose and of message. Change takes place in time and is often the result of the cumulative impacts of messy interventions. We strive for consistency and I hope that this chapter will help make that more of a reality; but we can survive lapses. We must not abandon smart plans because we have a bad day or something unexpected happens.

Summary

This chapter is about developing consistent responses to behavioral incidents. Developing these responses starts with getting clear what we want to achieve by having a response. A number of outcomes might be important:

- to effect safety

- to teach the individual about how the world is going to work from now on, what leads to what – what consequnces the behavior leads to

- to teach the individual about how other people are impacted by the behavior

- to teach the individual about how other people will view him

- to teach the person 'a lesson'.

Interventions for change can target behavioral change and/or cognitive change. They include:

- stopping the reinforcement for the behavior

- positively redirecting

- giving explanations

- tagging behaviors with concepts that are important to the individual

- levying costs.

These elements can be combined and we try to develop a script that we follow consistently when an incident occurs.

Interventions for safety involve:

- responding to escalation (distracting, calming, positively redirecting, using authoritarian control)
- responding to behavior (doing nothing, clearing the area, moving the person, calling for support, blocking and breaking away, holding the person).

We combine these elements into a detailed plan of what we do at each stage of an incident.

Ideas to think more about

Write down here any ideas taken from this chapter that you think might help your child.

PART 2

Themes and Supports

Part 2 gets into the specifics of behavioral work – the things that we can do to make things better based on our understanding of why the behavior occurs. It is organized in terms of common themes in behavior – what behavior tends to be about. Each chapter describes a specific theme and the kinds of work that will address the meaning of the behavior, its theme. Each chapter will suggest several ways of working with a theme (for example, activities to try, experiences to provide, skills to teach, ways to organize the environment, ways of getting information across, how to directly encourage or discourage behaviors). There is space at the end of each chapter for writing down ideas that might be helpful to the particular individual(s) with whom the reader is concerned.

Chapter 4

I Can't Stand That

Some behaviors are about reacting to a specific trigger that the individual finds physically uncomfortable or stressful.

> Every time Judith was around a baby and the baby screamed, Judith would attack the baby.

> If people got too close to Rick and touched him he would immediately bang his head with his fist.

> Whenever people around him coughed, Sam would hit them.

> Randy's parents had learned to sneak up on him in the night to cut his hair, as any attempt to cut his hair in the day led to incredible confrontations with Randy becoming very agitated and violent.

> Whenever teachers pointed out a mistake in Mike's work he would become very angry and spit or head butt.

The behavior, whatever its form, is about trying to relieve the discomfort of, block, get rid of or get away from the stimulus. The experience of discomfort for the individual seems to be intense and thus the need for action is urgent. The most common sources of such discomfort are particular noises or touches, but there are also more social discomforts (being talked at too much, being corrected) and some clear phobias (for example, dogs).

There has been much discussion in recent years about the sensory difficulties that people with autism experience. The things that most people regard as ordinary sensory experiences can trigger intense discomfort for people with autism. It is important to understand that at this stage we have no clear understanding as to why this should be so. There are a number of theoretical possibilities, but there is no evidence that supports one theory or the other. Such intolerances are also part of every human-being's experiences. It is important not to get too impressed by any one particular theory, but to cast around for practical techniques that might be helpful in dealing with these situations, wherever the ideas come from.

One of the themes of this book is to learn from the individual. In this case we need to check whether there are discomforts that the person experiences but deals with in a way that others would regard as 'constructive', not involving aggression, self-injury or any other kind of dangerous behavior. Exercise 4.1 helps with that.

Review Exercise 4.1 and see if it suggests any ways of working to help the person deal with the most intense situations. It is always quicker if we can find an approach that already works in one situation and apply it to another. One of the difficulties for people with autism is that they can come up with some smart ways of dealing with situations but do not automatically make the links to another situation that other people would regard as similar. One of the vital supports you can provide is to make these links and connections.

If this exercise does not suggest a way forward there are a number of common approaches to helping the person either be less troubled by particular stimuli or be able to respond more constructively when he does experience discomfort (in other words, cope better).

Avoid situations

There has to be a good reason for exposing people to things that they find highly aversive. Most of us organize our adult lives so that we are not needlessly exposed to the things that we find unpleasant. We cannot avoid all discomfort but we certainly do not court it, unless of course we are volunteering for some kind of 'reality' TV show. Most sane human beings do not believe in the deeply held British cultural notion that somehow discomfort and unpleasantness are 'character building'!

We can distinguish two levels of avoidance, outlined below.

Total avoidance

At this level of avoidance, we try to organize life so that there is no direct exposure to the aversive stimulus – before proceeding we always check the parks for dogs and the supermarkets for babies. We go outside the house to

Exercise 4.1 Management of discomfort

List all the things that your child finds uncomfortable, rate how intense the discomfort is and list how your child deals with the discomfort.

Things that cause discomfort	Level of discomfort usually experienced	Ways she deals with the discomfort

cough. We never vacuum when our child is at home and we never go to the hairdresser's. Total avoidance is often impossible to achieve (dogs, babies and coughing are everywhere). Even if we can achieve it, the cost may be high. It means limiting life and experiences and opportunities (we end up never going to restaurants or sports games, on buses or planes). It can just be too exhausting – bringing up a son or daughter with autism is tiring enough without having to get up in the night to cut hair and nails. However, it is always an approach to consider. There is no reason to feel guilty about avoidance as it is the most natural human response and we all use it to some extent. The questions to ask are:

- can complete avoidance be achieved?
- what are the costs of achieving it now?
- what are the costs if we have to keep up the avoidance long term?

A less draconian approach to avoidance is reasonable accommodation.

Reasonable accommodation

Here we use our understanding of the person's difficulties to devise a way of getting through important situations without triggering intense discomfort. We make an accommodation which enables the situation to occur but recognizes the person's difficulty. For example:

> It was understood that Mike was hypersensitive to certain words ('no', 'wrong') and that he was incredibly independent in learning and problem solving. It was reasonable to work out a script for correcting Mike that avoided the words 'no' and 'wrong' (for example, 'you need to look at that again', 'you need to redo that one', 'you need to check that one against the standards list'). It was also reasonable to find some problem-solving aids that would help Mike self-correct.

> Rick's sensitivity to touch was about light touch and touch to certain body areas (his back in particular) and was mainly when people initiated touch with him. He would sometimes initiate physical contact and as long as it was under his control he coped fine. It was therefore made part of Rick's support plan that we only use firm hand touch (hand-shakes, high-fives) with him as he was comfortable with this, and avoid imposing all other physical contact on him.

In making a reasonable accommodation, the questions to ask are:

- is there an accommodation that works?

- how easy it to use that accommodation? This is the question about the accommodation itself not about people's willingness to implement the accommodation. Complex accommodations will be hard to implement no matter how willing people are

- how viable is it to get that accommodation into all the situations where it is needed, now and into the future?

If there is an easy, effective accommodation which will cover all or most of the key situations then this is clearly an option to consider. Otherwise we need to consider other approaches as alternatives to or in combination with 'reasonable accommodation'.

Work with the individual to develop a coping strategy

This approach accepts that the individual will be exposed to situations that are unpleasant and looks to give her skills that will get her through these situations without doing anything dangerous. There are four main kinds of coping strategies:

1. sensory blocking
2. movement control
3. self-calming
4. communication.

Sensory blocking

We can work with the person to use something that will block out the aversive sensory input. This is easiest with noise sensitivities. The use of headphones, personal music systems and earplugs can all help in getting the individual through difficult situations. They do not necessarily block the input altogether but they dampen it and, in the case of the music systems, provide a distraction.

> In the early stages of working with Sam his parents bought him a very expensive set of noise-dampening headphones that could also be hooked to a music system. When going into situations where people might cough he was given the choice of wearing the headphones with or

without music and this helped him cope better when people coughed (he still found it aversive but he coped).

Most sensory blocking work focuses on sound but some people are very sensitive to aromas and the provision of some kind of alternative preferred aroma (a dab on the wrist, an impregnated tissue or pad that is carried around) can be helpful in these cases.

Movement control

The behaviors that give cause for concern usually involve some kind of gross body movement – hitting someone, hitting oneself, running off. They often happen very fast in response to the unpleasant stimulus. Teaching the person to do something physically incompatible to the behavior in the situation (standing still, clasping hands, sitting on hands) will help to disrupt the sequence and give a chance for another coping strategy to be used (such as self-calming or communication).

> Sam learned not only to use his headset when going into situations where people might cough, but was also taught to 'freeze' and lock his hands together whenever he heard a cough.

Self-calming

The third coping strategy is self-calming where the aim is to stop the build-up in agitation or emotional arousal that is triggered by the sensory stimulus. Behavioral outbursts often occur at a high point in arousal and if the arousal build-up can be stopped then the behavior will not occur. Self-calming strategies usually combine some kind of direct calming element with distraction. Examples include the following.

- *Breathing exercises* – learning to use slow, deep breathing.

- *Hand exercises* – learning to use things like squeeze balls, strong elastic bands or some simple self-massage techniques (squeezing down the arms, massaging the temples).

- *Aroma inhalation* – some aromas such as lavender can have a calming effect.

- *Repetitive sound* – whether this is a guru chanting 'Om', a psychologist babbling 'calm and relaxed', leaves falling in the Amazon forest or whales singing Handel's *Messiah* thousands of feet down off the coast of Alaska, repetition is at the heart of many calming interventions.

- *Eating* – comfort eating is exactly what it says. Eating tends to inhibit or reduce anxious feelings and other feelings of discomfort. Of course, there is a health dimension to this and we do live in an era of health fascism. But do not discount this much-enjoyed and simple approach to feeling better – 'let them eat chocolate'!!

Sam was taught as part of his coping strategy to take three deep breaths after he had locked his hands when someone coughed.

Most calming strategies involve three simple elements – reducing stimulation, slowing down, doing something repetitively. Many people with autism have devised for themselves good blocking, repetitive activities that we tend to define as self-stimulation and indeed pathologize by including them in the diagnostic criteria for autism. One of the problems is the slowing down element – people know how to rock, jump and weave their hands in front of their eyes, all potentially hypnotic and calming. What they are not so good at is slowing down, so the more agitated they get the faster and harder they jump, rock and hand weave, and this tends to feed into the escalation spiral. One alternative to consider is not to teach a new set of calming skills; rather, to try to help your son or daughter to use their own strategy, but to learn to slow it down when they are under pressure – teach them to slow rock, slow jump, slow weave.

The other element in calming is often some kind of distraction, switching the focus of your mind so that the disturbing stimulus is not so salient. People with autism often have activities that will focus them intensely and for long periods of time; again, these are often pathologized as 'obsessions'. They can be very useful distracters in aversive situations.

Judith loved putting items in the cart and pushing the cart in supermarkets. She was also a great Game Boy enthusiast. As long as she kept busy during the shopping trip and then had her Game Boy whilst waiting at the checkout line, she did not lose control if a baby cried.

If your child can calm himself down then implementing this approach usually involves making sure the necessary materials are available and then prompting their use in the situations where the stress arises.

If it is a question of teaching a new self-calming strategy then this is a longer-term matter. It means doing a lot of teaching away from the problematic situation – teaching breathing techniques, teaching self-massage, teaching use of squeeze balls and elastic, teaching use of aroma or listening to calming sounds. Sometimes this learning may take place as part of a broader program of work – learning yoga or going through sensory integration therapy. These are great skills to learn and potentially have many long-term advantages. However, all new learning takes time and the skills have to be practiced to fluency before they can be used effectively in stressful situations. It is certainly a great choice to make but set your sights on months or years of work – don't be discouraged if the squeeze ball does not work first time in the supermarket when the baby screams!

Communication

The fourth approach to coping is using communication skills. Here the focus is teaching the person to use a communicative skill as a means of getting the problematic situation resolved. The relevant messages will be about 'help me' or 'I want to go now'. This might involve teaching new skills or helping the individual use skills she already possesses but does not think to use in the situation.

> Sam was quite capable of asking to leave a situation that he did not like. However, he never actually did so. He needed practice and prompting to include in his coping strategy that he should ask to leave if his blocking, locking and calming strategies were not working well enough for him to stay safe.

If the individual does not already have the necessary skills then these will need to be taught and this will take time. It means:

- identifying a communication message that would likely be effective in managing the problematic situations

- identifying a medium for delivering this message, based on the skills for communication that the person already has (this may be speech, signs, pointing to a card, pressing a button on a 'talker')

- identifying the point at which the communication should be used. This will usually be as emotions are escalating. Many people with autism are not good at judging their emotional state. They may need others to cue them/give feedback as to when they are getting upset, and we might want to use a visual analog to indicate increasing upset (there is the popular, 'how fast is your engine running' approach, using a car speedometer analogy; you could also use temperature analogies or balloon inflating analogies – whatever you think would get through to your child that her upset is increasing and she needs to communicate)

- teaching to use the skill as the situations arise or to teach the skill in role play/drama/simulation situations, making sure that competent communication always works to make things better.

This is a very powerful way of coping with aversive situations but it will take time before the person becomes fully confident and fluent in the skill. However, once she has that skill it is a tremendous resource for the future as many challenging behaviors arise in situations that the individual finds unpleasant and wants to get out of.

Teaching coping strategies means that difficult situations are not avoided and that therefore the individual is repeatedly exposed to them, which turns out to be a very good thing in terms of the aversiveness of the situation being reduced.

Reduce the aversiveness of the situation

This can be effected in a two major ways:

1. experiencing control
2. repeated exposure.

Experiencing control

Many intolerances arise in situations where a sensory experience occurs in a way that is not under the control of the individual. It may come as a 'surprise' or it may just be the very fact that it is not under control that triggers the aversiveness. Control is a very important theme in many people's lives. Sometimes just giving the experience of control is enough to reduce the aversiveness of the experience when it occurs more naturally. Thus learning to use and control the vacuum cleaner, the blender, the ice maker, will help the individual tolerate other people using these things. This can expand to the use of communication skills; learning that you can ask people not to talk too much, that you can give the dog instructions that it follows, also gives a sense of control and reduces the panic of being trapped in a situation that you cannot control.

Repeated exposure

One of the stunning capabilities of the human being is that we can get used to almost anything, no matter how unpleasant it is. If we are repeatedly exposed to things that initially trigger strong negative feelings, then the strength of those feelings tends to decrease over time, provided that nothing really terrible happens during the exposure. For example, the more you are around dogs the less frightened you will become – unless, of course, a dog bites you. It does not always work but as a general rule repeatedly, safely exposing your child to the trigger situation is a good way of making it more tolerable. This is especially likely if the exposure starts small and gradually builds up. However, even if we cannot always do the small steps approach, repeated exposure may still lead to a reduction in experienced unpleasantness.

> Randy hated having his hair cut. It was managed because he had a hairdresser who loved him and would offer an appointment when no-one else would be in the salon. But it remained a huge and exhausting battle and he was getting bigger and stronger as his parents grew older and weaker. Soon it would no longer be possible for Randy to have his hair cut outside of his home. The family was able to get some additional help from a local agency and decided to tackle this by increasing the frequency of hair cuts using the agency's staff for additional hands-on support. It started essentially as a commando operation but with an icon sequence and a donut-related activity after the hair cut! After several well-executed trips Randy began to relax a little (he never got to enjoy it) and within three months he could be taken for a hair cut just by his mum and dad, using only verbal and icon prompting. A year later he was positively enjoying it and did not need such detailed preparation.
>
> Randy also hated any interference in his mouth. It was impossible to brush his teeth and all dental work had to be carried out under general anesthetic. Randy's dad decided this issue had to be confronted. He started work exposing Randy to having his teeth brushed every evening. He used an icon sequence (Randy was familiar with icons) and started just with putting toothpaste on the brush and holding it near Randy's mouth and then finishing. Gradually over time the icon sequence got longer and the toothbrush got into the mouth for longer and longer. After six months Randy was tolerating a reasonable amount of tooth brushing and was starting to take over and do it for himself. Randy got a new dentist who was very understanding and keen to find a way of not always having to use a general anesthetic for dental work. She offered Randy an appointment every two weeks and again started just by him coming, then looking around, then sitting in the chair, then having his

teeth brushed. After a further six months Randy had his first full dental examination, including x rays, and coped just fine. A year later he had some minor work carried out on his teeth and more is planned soon.

Randy's story illustrates the range of approaches to exposure. Ideally a graded approach is preferred (as with the teeth). Even better, a more technical version of graded exposure known as 'systematic desensitization' can sometimes be used.

> After Sam had begun work on his coping strategies an heroic group of staff went about some systematic desensitization with Sam. It was known that both loudness and type of cough contributed to Sam's discomfort. Tape recordings were made of various types of cough starting with low provocation coughs and building up. These were played to Sam during the course of his day starting at low volume and with low provocation coughs. If he did not hit anyone after exposure he was rewarded with a candy ('cough candy' as it was jokingly known). The exposure on tape was gradually built up and then the team switched to 'live exposure' with them coughing but following the same graded approach. Sam certainly became more tolerant of coughing.

However, this kind of precision control is not always possible in the real world and it is important to understand that exposure is a robust intervention especially if the exposure is reasonably frequent and if some control over the level of exposure is possible. The situations to avoid are ones where something even worse does happen (the dog bites!) or where the individual becomes so aroused that he loses complete control. Repeated exposure leading to low or moderate discomfort will generally lead to increased tolerance.

Use reinforcement

Randy's hair-cut story illustrates the use of rewards as part of the process of building tolerance. The issue of reinforcement is, however, one that is very important for all the approaches to building coping and tolerance that we have discussed. We need to ask how we can get over to the person that we thought it was wonderful the way that she:

- used her blocking strategy
- used her self-calming strategy
- used her communication strategy
- coped with that horrible situation and did not lash out, run out or self-injure.

To do this we need to identify the reinforcers that are meaningful to the person – from praise to special hand shakes to donuts to computer time. We then have to organize things so that success is quickly followed by one of these events. People need to hear in whatever way works for them how great they have been, what skills they have demonstrated, what courage they have shown. We are asking people to do something difficult and deal differently with a situation which from their point of view they already have a good way of dealing with. Motivation is a critical element and by making sure that we reinforce competence and courage we make sure that people will be more likely to persevere and keep using their newfound ways of coping.

Intolerances that come and go

The kinds of discomforts and intolerances that we have been discussing some-times have a time-limited period of existence – they are there for a time, then they go never to be seen again. Some may be longer term – we may never get to the point where Randy really enjoys going to the dentist. Others tend to come and go. They are very prominent for a time, disappear and then resurface at a later date.

Sometimes they resurface because of traumatic events. Having learned to tolerate dogs the individual gets bitten. Having learned to cope with babies crying one day there is a baby with a particularly high-pitched scream that goes on for a long time and the individual cannot get away and loses control. However, the most common reason for this 'cycling' of intolerances is a shift in underlying state. This is perfectly understandable from a common sense point of view. We cope with a lot of discomfort in our lives if we are feeling in generally good shape (we feel well and happy). But if we are tired, in pain, stressed, then every little thing bugs us, we focus more on the negative things and we cannot distract ourselves so easily from them. We are much more ready to explode. Thus the return of intolerances will sometimes be a sign of an underlying state change. If that is the case – and there will be other signs of this – then it is important to focus on changing the underlying negative state rather than tackling the intolerances directly. Chapter 12 looks at practical ways of restoring a sense of well-being. Once the state is shifted the intolerances may fade and not need further attention. If they do not fade then they will need the kinds of attention described in this chapter; but this is now more likely to succeed than if we try to address them when the person has lost his overall sense of well being.

Specific therapies

There are some specific therapies that make claims to address the sensory difficulties that many people with autism seem to experience. The two best known are sensory integration therapy and auditory integration therapy. Whether a family pursues these therapies is a family decision. If they are not readily available and getting access to them is going to require a significant investment of family resources then the following thoughts may be helpful in making a family decision.

- We have as yet no understanding of the basis for the sensory difficulties reported by and for people with autism. All theories are speculative. Research on these sensory therapies is limited and to date has not been very supportive of their likely benefits in terms of sensory processing. However, no group study can ever answer whether all individuals benefit or otherwise. It is possible for a study to show that a group of people identified as autistic do not show benefit in general but one individual may have. Who is to say if your child is like the individual who benefited or the majority who did not?

- The intervention might have a stand-alone value. It might be fun for the child and have other benefits even if it does not resolve intolerances. Sensory integration therapy certainly scores well on the fun factor.

- Accessing the therapies may cost time, effort and money and it will be useful to identify what will be sacrificed if you choose to invest in a therapy.

- Finally, this chapter has described the simpler, low-tech, everyday approaches to helping with intolerances – do these seem just as likely to help your child as the branded therapies?

It is a huge challenge for families with autism to decide what paths to follow for their child. All around are claims for miracles and massive effects…if you follow the particular path recommended by the claimant. It is hard to choose between these paths, especially as claimants tend to deride the claims of others. Every professional has an axe to grind and a vested interest. An important message of this book to families is *use your head and trust your heart!*

Summary

The problem addressed

Behaviors that are triggered by stimuli that generate large feelings of discomfort for the person with autism.

Approaches described

- total avoidance
- reasonable accommodations
- teaching blocking skills
- teaching self-calming skills
- teaching communication skills
- giving control experiences
- setting up controlled, repeated exposure
- reinforcing competence and courage
- addressing underlying well-being issues
- specific therapies.

Ideas to think more about

Write down here any ideas taken from this chapter that you think might help your son or daughter.

Chapter 5

You've Lost Me

There are a cluster of everyday situations that are a great challenge for many people with autism. These include changing activities, when they are supposed to stop doing one thing and refocus on another. Major transitions in the day (such as home to school or work in the morning, work or school to home in the afternoon) are another challenge. Waiting times – those in-between times when they have stopped doing one thing and will be doing another – can be difficult. Likewise unstructured times, when they are supposed to think of something to do for themselves (such as recess time at school, before dinner at home, going shopping for the family).

> Mark enjoyed watching his cartoons and loved eating his dinner but when he had to shift from one to the other he became very angry and aggressive.

> Getting Rodney off to school in the morning was always a fraught affair and a time when he was very likely to get loud and upset, and start hitting himself and attacking others.

> Jalisa loved going to McDonald's but the journey there was always a worry because if the car had to stop at a light or junction she would become very upset and start hitting herself.

> Dwayne coped very well during lessons at his mainstream school but when it came to recess he would sit on the floor and rock, the other children would begin to tease him and he would then get angry and attack them.

> Joe was fine during supermarket shopping if he was kept busy with things to fetch and put in the trolley, but if there was a line at the checkout he would become very upset and attack other customers.

Although these are common scenarios, the actual mechanisms involved in them are quite varied. People with autism can find it hard to shift their attention. They are good at focusing on a single topic but when it comes time to move on they find it hard to let go the current focus and shift attention to another topic. They can also find it hard to hold more than one idea at a time in their minds, which creates difficulty with making choices and also leads to problems in holding sequences of events, especially if one of the events is very significant. Once the focus is on school or McDonald's or getting back into the car, then that is all that is understood, not the steps leading up to it. Thus, if it does not happen right away a lot of frustration is generated. Lack of imagination can be another problem so that when an individual is required to think up something to do or make a choice, options and possibilities do not readily flash up. This can itself lead to upset or to switching over to 'screen-saver' mode (Dwayne rocking). The problem of lack of imagination also interferes with most forms of problem solving, when a situation is not routine and the individual is left to work out what to do. If a focus is not found (as with the screen-saver option), then the individual can start to become overwhelmed by environmental stimulation, which would normally be blocked by the central focus for attention. Unstructured times can be noisy and chaotic and if the individual cannot fix his mind on to something specific then he becomes wide open to all the stimulation around and gets overwhelmed and distressed. The difficulties in all these situations are based on cognitive differences – they reflect how minds work and information is processed.

However, a transition is often more than just a cognitive activity. It involves more than just a shift of mental focus from one thing to another. There is also an emotional component. Transitions often generate an emotional 'spike'. This is most obvious for the major transitions in a day (getting up, getting to work/school, getting home in the late afternoon/evening). Most people generate rituals around these times that are about settling down and focusing after the physical transition has been made. Close examination may reveal similar settling rituals during smaller transitions in the day, when we switch from one activity to another (a sort of ready–set–go process). Many people with autism are not good at monitoring or recognizing their own emotional states and are not very good at managing the feelings they do recognize. This leaves them vulnerable to the emotional spikes at transitions. Either the spike itself is large and overwhelming or there is a cumulative effect after several transitions.

The behaviors that occur in these varied contexts may simply be a reflection of an overaroused, distressed state. Under this kind of emotional pressure behaviors that are normally inhibited become disinhibited and the individual starts injuring himself, attacking others, throwing and breaking things, jumping and screaming, being verbally abusive. In other words, the individual loses control. The behaviors themselves do not serve any specific purpose, they are just part of a very distressed state.

However, the behaviors can also serve a purpose. They can sometimes be an effective means of bringing about a change that strengthens the behaviors. They are functional and lead to something that is important happening for the individual. For example, the individual may get into the car or to McDonald's quicker, may be given an activity that she likes to do and that calms her down, may get taken to a quieter area that is more comfortable for her, may get the close support of a trusted person.

The common thread in this chapter is that the individual may be acting problematically because he lacks a clear understanding of what is going on and is not focused in a way that will enable appropriate behavior – he is lost, confused, disoriented and may be getting increasingly distressed by this experience. The underlying mechanisms, however, are varied and this opens up a range of interventions, determined by what we see as the main issues for the specific individual about whom we are concerned.

The approach throughout the book emphasizes the importance of using what we have learned works and does not work for the individual, as well as more theoretical views of what the problem might be. Exercise 5.1 (p.66) tries to draw out this practical knowledge.

Additional ideas will be generated when we look at the things that we can do that address the underlying difficulties described earlier.

Enable attentional shifting

If we think that part of the difficulty is that the person finds it hard to shift focus and gets upset when this is required, there are a number of interventions that may help.

Exercise 5.1 Contributors to success in difficult situations

The first step is to list the situations (transitions, unstructured times, mornings, evenings, waiting times) in which things often go badly from a behavioral point of view. Next to these, list similar situations that often go quite well – when there is less likelihood of behaviors occurring (they may occur sometimes but not often). When we compare the two lists, we may get some ideas about what makes the difference – what it is that makes those similar situations go well. This in turn may generate some ideas about how to improve the situations that are currently difficult.

Situations in which things often go badly	*Similar situations in which things often go well*

Ideas for changing the approach to difficult situations:

Practicing interruptions

This is a way of helping the individual cope more easily with attentional shifts, reducing the amount of upset that they generate. It is like the approaches described in Chapter 4. We look at the situations in which problems occur and see if there is opportunity to break up the attentional focus without triggering a meltdown. For example in the case of Mark, described at the beginning of this chapter, we could practice sneaking up on him and playfully surprising him or doing something outrageous to create a distraction during cartoon time. We could introduce small amounts of snack that we place just out of reach so Mark has to actually do something to get them. The challenge is to create attentional disruptions without overwhelming Mark emotionally. This will serve to teach Mark to adapt emotionally to attentional disruption which in turn may make the 'big' transition from cartoon to dinner a little easier.

Expanding the information available to the individual about activity sequences

Here we try to make obvious the activity sequence for the time period in which problems occur, so that the individual is not just focused on what he is doing now but has some idea about what happens next. We would also want to help the individual know what choices are available when it is up to her to decide what she is going to do.

Throughout the book there will be a lot of reference to the use of visual communication as a means of enhancing understanding. This has been one of the biggest developments in support for people with autism since the early 1970s – the realization that we can often get information through more effectively if we present it in a different way. For many people with autism, even those with good speech, visual processing is better than auditory processing or is a preferred medium because it involves less social pressure, less sequential processing and is less dependent on speed. Thus, putting information into a visual format can be a very powerful way of enhancing the person's understanding and enabling the splitting of attention. The work of Division TEACCH, Carol Gray's Social Stories™, and Bondy and Frost's PECS approach are all examples of this realization.

Using the example of Mark again, in order to help him cope with the shift we could use a board that lays out the evening's sequence from top to bottom. Mark works well with visual icons but others may do better with a written checklist or a photo sequence. Mark works best with sequences no more than

5–7 items long. On his evening board are two activities before cartoons, then cartoons, dinner and two activities after dinner. As an activity finishes Mark peels off the icon and posts it away (in a plastic pouch on the sequence board) and moves on to the next activity. The board is hung close to the TV during cartoon time and when it is time to move on Mark is prompted to turn off the TV, post the icon away and sit down for dinner (the sequence board is moved to be near where he sits).

These kinds of interventions are not quick fixes. It takes time to find the best way of presenting information and perseverance to use it day in day out before it becomes a useful tool. However, it is a very powerful tool. It gives better quality information, it helps to split and shift attention and it gives a greater sense of control. It is also interactive (things have to be checked off, icons removed) and this provides a transition ritual, an important element that will be discussed in more detail later.

Giving warnings

From the individual's point of view a requirement for transition may come as a surprise. If the person has the capacity to lock attention to one thing and exclude all else then this certainly means that she gets more out of the focus of attention but it cripples her ability to 'multitask'. Some people can truly multitask. Most people have a focus of attention but also process other cues from the environment so that they have some sense of what is going on around them and what they will be doing next. Being highly focused means that you do not pick up any warning signs that things are about to move on – hence the surprise experience.

One way of making transitions easier is to give very clear and obvious warnings that things are about to change. This can be done in a number of ways. We can give spoken warnings ('In a few minutes we will be having dinner', perhaps saying this two or three times before the transition actually occurs). We can use a timer set to go off ahead of the transition or something that plays a set 'jingle'. We can use visual warnings, for example using a picture traffic light sequence stuck on to the sequence board to warn of the upcoming change (this could be helpful in Mark's case). The transition occurs after the green light is stuck on the board. Ready–set–go is a useful mantra for giving warnings, whether they are given in words, in pictures or by devices.

It is important to repeat that none of these interventions is likely to solve the problem instantly. Over time (weeks and months) the trauma of transition will decline so that there may be some grumpiness and protest but not the major behavioral outbursts which were the original focus of our concern.

Making choices concrete

Times when the individual has to make up his own mind what to do or is asked to make a choice of some kind can be difficult. It helps to spell out the choices available and to represent them in a way that makes them accessible. The principle of 'going visual' is again helpful – put out the cereal packets or lay out the activities in front of him, use a choice board with pictures or words stuck on to the board.

> Dwayne was provided with a set of activity cards (showing options of what to do in recess) and a daily schedule giving him the times of recess. He was taught how to plan what he wanted to do during each recess (select the activity, write it in on his schedule). By externalizing something that other people do 'in the head', Dwayne became able to make choices about how to spend his 'free' time other than sitting and rocking.

Many of the approaches described here do more than enable attention shifting, they also give the individual more understanding of what is going on or what is expected. It is a lack of detailed understanding that can contribute to the difficulties described in this chapter.

Improve detailed understanding

So much information in daily life is not spelled out, it is inferred. It is only when we meet people whose minds are more exact than our own that this issue is revealed. These are the people who are outraged when someone says 'let's get on the bus and go swimming' and they do not find a pool on the bus. They are outraged when told 'let's drive to McDonald's' and the car then stops at red lights. They are stunned to find that although it was said 'we'll get the shopping and then we'll go home' in fact when we have got the shopping we stand in a line of people and do nothing. They are mortified when the teacher asks a question, says 'what is the answer?' and when they call out the answer they then get told off because what was meant was that after the question, you put up your hand if you know the answer and if the teacher chooses you then you speak, but otherwise you do not speak.

If this is an issue contributing to the behavioral outbursts there are a number of approaches that will help.

- *Be specific* – one of the golden rules of support for people with autism is that we cannot be too specific. If we are going to explain something verbally make sure that we are precise in what we tell someone. If we are going to explain it visually make sure we cover all the steps. If there is any doubt, be more specific.

- *Give information in an accessible form* – as discussed above, many people with autism find it easier to access information through the visual channel – photos, icons, line drawings, written messages, checklists. This can apply even to people who appear to have very good spoken language and verbal understanding.

- *Keep the information salient* – information needs not just to be available but to be attended to. Given the attentional styles of many people with autism, helping them to attend to socially relevant information can be a considerable challenge.

Taking the above three points together gives us three questions to consider.

1. What does the person need to know – what is the critical information that he needs and is not getting?

2. How can I present that information – what medium works best?

3. How do I keep the information salient?

Rodney needs to know that he gets up, gets dressed, has breakfast, brushes his teeth, plays until the bus horn sounds when he gets his backpack and goes.

Jalisa needs to know that we drive in the car, keep busy, stop at red lights and stop signs and get to McDonald's.

Joe needs to know that we go in the supermarket, get our things, stand in line and keep busy, go through the checkout, get back in the car and go home.

Rodney and Jalisa can relate to icon sequences, Joe can read.

For Rodney we keep the information salient by having a sequence board and each time an activity is finished he peels of the icon and posts it away. We help him by having his backpack next to the front door. We have to think about what he can play when he is waiting and have an icon that represents the activity (Rodney likes to flick through catalogs, play with string and play on a keyboard). We add to the salience of the bus horn by having a 'talker' device that Rodney is prompted to press when the horn sounds and that speaks the message (time to get on the bus for school).

We keep the information salient for Jalisa by taking her through the icon sequence before we get in the car, fixing the icons on the seat ahead of her when she is riding and verbally warning her when we are going to stop at a light or junction. We make sure that we have something in the car that she can play with while she is riding (she loves Polly Pockets).

For Joe we keep the information salient by providing a written checklist that he takes into the supermarket and checks off items as they are completed. We also carry with us an activity for him to do while standing in line (he loves his Game Boy) so that his mind is kept focused on what he needs to do at every stage.

The examples above all illustrate problems in understanding that are about events and their sequences. Yet often the lack of understanding is about social rules – what is the appropriate way to behave in class, at recess, at a friend's house, in the supermarket? The behaviors that we find challenging may feel very natural to the person himself – it seems natural to call out an answer, to tease other people at recess, to wander off from a friend and busy yourself with something that interests you, to run around the supermarket sweeping things off the shelves. Most social situations are governed by unwritten and unspoken rules and people with autism may be blissfully unaware of these rules. They behave in ways that feel natural to them but that others define as problematic.

There are two approaches that help to make rule-based information accessible.

1. Clarify rules directly

It can be very helpful to establish a set of rules for specific situations – house rules, class rules, supermarket rules, recess rules, sidewalk rules, bus rules. We should try to state the rules in positive terms. For example, 'We use our hands to touch each other gently' rather than 'Don't hit'; 'In the supermarket we use our indoor voice' rather than 'Don't scream'. Positive statementing is better suited to the thinking styles of many people with autism. Negative rules require the person to work out for herself what she should do instead and, as we have seen, that kind of mental operation can be a great challenge for people with autism. Of course this is not an absolute requirement and we will use some negative rules; but if we are going to do that we should make sure that the negatively stated rules are outnumbered by the positively stated rules.

The number of rules per situation should be limited (three to five is a rough guideline). The rules should be put into a concrete 'external' format (think Ten Commandments, tablets of stone…not literally of course!!). They may be written in words or represented by icons or pictures, color coding can be added to indicate positive and negative rules. The rules should be posted and regularly presented (for example, before bus trips or supermarket visits).

They should be brought into prominence when we are encouraging the individual to stop engaging in a behavior that has been identified as problematic. Instead of saying 'Don't…' we say 'Remember the house/bus/class rule is…' as we point to the posted list of rules.

2. Hang rule information onto personally meaningful hooks

Rules are a powerful source of information and fit in well with the way that the minds of many people with autism work. They bring clarity and simplification. Sometimes, however, the information that they contain can only be absorbed if the rules are hung on a 'hook' that has particular relevance for the individual.

> Jerry was a tall guy in his late teens who could talk well and had some basic reading and writing skills. In the classroom and structured community activities he functioned well but in less formal situations in the community his interest in women would overwhelm him and he would approach strangers asking for a hug and inviting them to his house. Although Jerry himself would not harm people under these circumstances he was certainly at risk of being harmed because of this behavior. A set of rules was formulated for him about ways to greet strangers, whom you could ask for a hug (family members plus a list of specific individuals) and whom he had to check with before inviting anyone to the house. Jerry understood these rules well, had no trouble remembering them but continued to make inappropriate approaches to people in the community. Concern was increasing and in the course of a conversation with Jerry about what was going on he suddenly said: 'Oh, you mean these things are "inappropriate".' Once we tagged the positive rules as 'appropriate' and his current behaviors as 'inappropriate' Jerry made no further mistakes in the community. Of course words like appropriate/inappropriate had long been used with Jerry but until that moment we had no idea that it had become an important organizing concept for him.

This question of hooks for information will come up again when we are dealing with extremely controlling behaviors (Chapter 9) and considering mood management (Chapter 10). It sets us the challenge of gaining insight into the person's own frame of reference and inserting important social information into that frame. The frame may be about certain words (as in Jerry's case), or certain people who have credibility (for example, doctors), including TV characters. It is a good lesson in humility to realize that Harry Potter and

Spongebob can be more credible sources of information than anyone else, but if that is what works for the individual then that is the way to go. As a general rule it is better to push on open doors than those that are locked and barred.

Social Stories™

Rules often appeal to people with autism – they are active seekers of social clarity. However, rules are relatively inflexible and do not teach any of the underlying reasons for the rules. They do not teach about how other people think and feel about things (key reasons as to why we control our impulses). A more comprehensive approach to building social understanding is the Social Stories work of Carol Gray. This is now well known and there are many published texts that both provide guidance on how to write Social Stories and that offer a lot of ready made Social Stories. It is another powerful way of helping people learn about how to manage difficult social situations, such as transitions and unstructured times, and how to develop good manners and other social skills.

Help people to keep busy during the 'gaps'

It is impossible to fill life completely with structured activities. There will be times when it is necessary to wait or to find something for yourself to do. These situations present considerable challenges for many people with autism. It is worth completing Exercise 5.2 (p.74).

If you complete Exercise 5.2, right away it will be clear that none of us 'does nothing'. We fill in the time with activities, thoughts and fantasies, social interactions of one sort or another. It is also clear that many of these situations have an emotional element – feelings of frustration, irritation, tension, restlessness. What we do to manage these situations is to find something to do that both fills the time and that brings us a degree of comfort. If we were not able to do this then these situations would easily become increasingly uncomfortable and this in turn might lead to bad behavior. Many service industries are very careful to actively manage these situations (opening additional checkout lines, serving drinks and snacks, bringing activities for the kids).

Our support for people with autism is merely helping them to access the things that the rest of us access at these difficult times. Earlier in this chapter we saw how Rodney, Jalisa and Joe were all given access to activities that help to hold their attention during waiting periods. The role of the family or workers was to ensure that these things were available and to prompt and

Exercise 5.2 Filling time

What do you do when you are:

- waiting in line at the supermarket?

- stuck in traffic and you need to get somewhere that is important to you?

- flying in an airplane?

- sitting on a bus or train?

encourage their use. Dwayne's case illustrated the teaching of specific skills: Dwayne became more capable at managing these situations for himself, without others actively supporting him. The approach that we take will depend upon the individual and the situations in which difficulties arise. However, the guiding principle is that we develop plans that help people to focus at unstructured times rather than hope that they will solve this for themselves. This will provide interest, avoid boredom, avoid people being overwhelmed by stimulation and prevent the build-up of uncomfortable emotions. This work illustrates that what we are trying to do is not just to help people at the mental level (giving them something to focus the mind on) but also at the emotional level (promoting positive feelings, reducing negative feelings). We earlier considered transitions just from the mental level – how to give people access to information that they can understand. We now look again at transitions, but this time from the emotional level.

Actively manage the emotional aspects of transitions

It has already been pointed out that transitions and unstructured times are often times of emotional escalation – this may be because of boredom, uncertainty, frustration at letting go an activity or because of overstimulation following a loss of focus. However, there are also some transitions which involve major shifts in biorhythmic functioning and human mood – getting up in the morning and getting into work or learning mode; going to bed at night, winding down and heading for sleep; and the late afternoon period when there is a downswing in energy and feelings of tiredness/irritability are coupled with a major activity transition such as coming home from school or work. It is not surprising that these major transitions in the day are often peak times for behavioral challenges.

The interventions already discussed certainly help to manage the more emotional aspects of transitions. They reduce uncertainty and provide focus. Sometimes, however, it may be necessary to look in more detail at how we optimize mood and emotional functioning during transitions and develop more comprehensive 'transition rituals', particularly for the big changes in the day outlined above. Doing Exercise 5.3 (p.76) will clarify this.

Surprisingly there is a lot of research into things that produce short-term changes in human mood but this research is rarely related to autism. Among the most prominent mood shifters are:

- ten minutes' brisk exercise (for increasing positive energy)
- repetitive activities (for calming)
- food (for calming)
- laughter (for fracturing negative emotions and lifting a mood)
- music (for calming or energizing)
- quiet time/time alone (for calming)
- massage (for calming and energizing).

There is also a lot of interest (but less research) in the use of aromas, with lavender and chamomile being touted for their relaxing properties.

It is noticeable that talking about things does not feature on the list of well-validated, short-term mood enhancers. Indeed, large amounts of language often act as a significant stressor for people with autism, even those with apparently good language skills. Silence may well be golden in terms of transition rituals.

Exercise 5.3 Personal rituals

Detail your preferred way of starting the day or coming back from work or settling down to sleep. What are the things that contribute to an ideal start to the day, an ideal transition to the evening, an ideal settling to sleep? Look in fine detail at all the things that you do during these times and particularly note those things that cause most discomfort if you miss them out or are unable to do them.

Preferred sequence of activities	Discomfort level if missed

The question is how to use this information to develop good rituals at the key transition points in the day. How might we use exercise, food, music, activities, jokes and fun, ambient stimulation, bodyworks and aromas to achieve the kind of mood outcomes that we are seeking (gradual energizing in the morning, calming and energizing in the late afternoon, calming in the lead-up to sleep)? Exercise 5.4 (p.78) will help to think through an ideal start to the day, afternoon transition and bed-time routine for the person with autism whose needs we are considering.

The ideas contained in this section are also relevant for managing other difficult transitions in the day when a lot of negative emotions are generated. As this is a relatively new area of work there are fewer clear case examples than we have been able to generate for other interventions. It features increasingly in my own work and there are certainly some special schools that incorporate these ideas into how lessons are started and ended.

Develop skills that are an alternative to the problematic behavior

Sometimes a behavior occurring at transition or unstructured times is an effective way of gaining access to something that relieves the problem – gaining access to a preferred person or activity or to a less stressful situation. Much of what we have discussed already helps to prevent these situations arising by keeping the person informed and oriented, by providing focus and maintaining comfort. However, not all situations can be planned for in this way and there will be times in life when situations arise when the individual has important concerns and needs a way of dealing with them, other than by direct action (bad behavior). The concerns themselves are reasonable (activity, quiet, support). It is the method of getting access that is unreasonable. If the person was able to communicate what he wanted in more socially acceptable ways then all would be well. These are examples where behavior is truly a form of communication and where the answer lies in teaching effective communicative alternatives. As this is the subject of the next chapter it will not be dealt with here.

In almost all the behavioral work that we do, motivation is critical. This applies to all human beings seeking to make a change. It is a particular issue for people with autism who may not see that their own behavior is a problem and may not see any particular benefit from doing things differently. Positive reinforcement is therefore an important tool in our supports.

Exercise 5.4 Designing ideal transition rituals

Use the ideas suggested in this section plus your own knowledge of your family and your child with autism to detail an ideal way of starting the day, coming home in the afternoon and settling off to sleep.

Starting the day	*Coming home in the afternoon*	*Settling off to sleep*

Now take a highlighter pen and mark those elements that you think you could manage to incorporate into most days in your family life.

Use reinforcement

Coping with transitions, unstructured times and waiting is a significant challenge for all human beings, but it is especially so for people with autism whose minds are not well adapted to these purposes. If people handle themselves well in these situations it is vital that we communicate to them how much we admire and appreciate what they have done. We need to identify the reinforcers that are meaningful to the person – from praise to special hand-shakes to donuts to computer time. We then have to organize things so that success is quickly followed by one of these events. People need to hear, in whatever way works for them, how great they have been, what skills they have shown, how smart they have been. We are asking people to do something difficult. Motivation is a critical element and by making sure that we reinforce often the successes people have we will ensure that that they will be more likely to persevere either with the strategies that they have some up with for themselves or with the strategies that we have been helping them to acquire.

Work on relationship building

Helping people in the ways described in this chapter depends upon us being effective at communicating with, advising and redirecting the person with autism. The person needs to be open to our influence. However, there can be times when we are not in that position, when the person with autism is not open to our influence and is engaged solely in following his own agenda without paying attention to other people. This is often seen when the children are very young and all early intervention programs strive to make other people psychologically salient to the child with autism. Social engagement is a fragile thing for people with autism and can be lost – people can slip away at any age and once they are out of engagement they are hard to help (and often increasingly challenging in their behavior). They often will not tolerate our physical presence, are absorbed deeply in their own self-generated behaviors, do not cooperate in activities we suggest and do not follow directions. If we are at that point – where we have little general influence over the person with autism – then, rather than working on the sorts of specific issues described in this chapter, we may need to go back to basics and establish a degree of social engagement. We will need to focus on relationship (re)building. Chapter 11, 'Loss of Social Connectedness', gives details on how to rebuild our personal engagement with an individual (pp.157–9). If you feel that the individual has lost their sense of social connectedness, you may find this section in Chapter 11 of vital importance.

Summary

The problem addressed

Behaviors that arise during transition, unstructured or waiting times. These can arise for a number of reasons including difficulty shifting attention, lack of understanding, boredom, loss of focus and overstimulation, emotional discomfort and behavior leading to access to preferred situations.

Approaches described

- enable attention shifting
  - practice interruptions
  - expand the information available to the individual about activity sequences
  - give warnings
  - make choices concrete
- improve detailed understanding
  - be specific
  - give information in an accessible form
  - keep information salient
  - clarify rules directly
  - hang rule information on to personally meaningful hooks
  - use Social Stories
- help people to keep busy during the gaps
- actively manage the emotional aspects of transitions
- develop skills that are an alternative to the problematic behavior
- use reinforcement
- work on relationship building.

Ideas to think more about

Write down here any ideas taken from this chapter that you think might help your child.

Chapter 6

There's Something
That I Want From You

Behavior in some situations is about persuading other people to do something specific for the individual. It is a very direct form of communication – the individual is saying 'I want you to do [this]...'

> Martin would sometimes become very upset in crowded noisy situations and start to grab, bite and push people until he was taken out to a quieter place... It was his way of saying 'Get me out of here'.

> Arnold would sometimes get very noisy and go round hitting people on the head and quite often he would be given some popcorn to 'calm him down'... He had learned that in his world the sign for popcorn was a heavy blow to the top of someone else's head!

> During 'free play' Simon would go round tipping over furniture and ripping things off the wall and only stop when someone gave him his favorite fiddly toys – he had learned to ask for his toys by damaging property.

> Sara would suddenly run off and those with her would then run after her (she loved 'chase') – 'absconding' was her way of saying 'let's play chase'.

> Carl would be outraged when people interrupted him and suggested that he do some work. He would punch his head very hard and often people would then let him get on with whatever he was doing – punching his head was his way of saying 'leave me alone'.

Not all communicative situations are as clear cut as this. Sometimes the behavior itself is not a direct communication but you can see that a communication skill might help to make the situation better.

> Catherine would get very upset when the computer crashed or would not do as she wanted. She would then hurl the screen to the ground. She was not really asking for help – she was just mad and doing the things that we all (secretly) want to do when computers screw up. However, if she asked someone for help when the computer crashed it would save a lot of money.

> When Junior got stressed he would start banging his head with his knee, banging his head on the floor and generally become very upset. He was not asking for someone to calm him down – he was being upset in the way that came naturally to him. If he could learn to ask for help when he got upset that might prevent the situation escalating and reduce the likelihood that Junior would harm himself.

If the behavior that concerns you is in part about these kinds of issues then there are three major strategies for addressing these issues, which we will examine in this chapter. In addition, for the specific situation of the individual communicating that he does not want to do what we are suggesting, I will describe a number of interventions additional to these three in the last section of this chapter.

Make whatever is needed readily available

People with disabilities often have access to their preferences controlled to a much greater degree than do other people. Their preferences may be regarded as 'treats' that they have to earn. Their preferences may be regarded as unhealthy or (age) inappropriate and access may be routinely denied. Disabilityland can be a Dickensian place.

> Maybe popcorn should be freely available to Arnold.

> Maybe Simon's twiddlers should be freely available during 'free play'.

> Maybe we could schedule playing chase with Sara several times a day anyway.

> Maybe we could work hard to comfort Junior at the first sign of upset anyway.

Making things freely available is not always possible. It is rarely a complete solution although it is often part of the solution. Sometimes it involves timing, as in the situations where there is a build-up – the individual has a problem, finds it upsetting and starts to get upset. Stepping in before the distress gets out of hand and the individual loses control will be helpful and this may involve providing what she wants or helping her in other ways to solve the problem. This is not rewarding bad behavior because it is done before there is any bad behavior. Getting upset is not bad behavior. Hitting people or harming oneself may be.

Be aware of the signs of upset, the common causes of upset and develop plans for stepping in early

In situations when the person gets upset it is sometimes possible to step in and reduce escalation so that behavioral incidents are avoided. This is not easy. It can be difficult to get in before things escalate out of hand. Warning signs can be missed or the intervention made is inappropriate – for example, we try to hug someone who does not like touch, we talk a lot to someone who is stressed by language input, we become bossy and authoritarian – and thus we escalate rather than calm the situation.

Dealing with these situations constructively is more likely if we develop a plan. For this kind of plan we will need to know the following.

- *The signs of upset* – these can be very individual – whistling, singing a certain song, asking a certain question, making a particular kind or noise. They can also be the common signs of upset – increased movement, increased vocalization or talking, crying, shouting.

- *The sorts of issues that commonly upset the individual* – again, these will be vary from person to person, will usually be well known to the family but may be less familiar to people working with the individual outside of the family.

- *Approaches that are effective in calming and settling the individual* – this will be either a combination of both solving the problem and bringing general arousal down or a focusing on just the calming on occasions when we do not understand the problem or cannot solve it right now. Tactics that effectively reduce arousal will vary and may include moving away to somewhere quiet, going for a walk, giving a back rub, offering a drink or snack, playing a particular piece of music or offering a repetitive activity.

A useful format for these plans was developed by Michael Smull as part of the process of person-centered planning. It is illustrated here using the case of Catherine, described earlier.

When Catherine...	We think it means...	And we will...
Cusses quietly in front of the computer	She is having difficulty doing what she wants	Go over and rub her shoulder
Gets louder and is starting to stamp	She is still frustrated about the computer	Try to sort out the problem with the computer
Is shouting and thumping the table	She is beginning to lose control	Suggest going outside for a walk and fixing the computer later

These kinds of plans are particularly helpful if, as parents, our stress levels tend to lead us to respond in ways that do not calm the situation. They are also helpful when we want to make sure that others who take care of our kids but do not necessarily know them that well can act effectively when they get upset. They also serve a less obvious purpose. They let the person know that we understand she has a problem and that we are concerned about that. We let her know that she is not alone. This is a vital challenge to the intrinsic isolating tendency of the condition that we call autism.

Getting in early is not always possible. It depends upon other people being present to observe signs, being sensitive to the signs and being available to step in. It leaves the individual dependent on other people. In order to empower significantly that person we need a longer-term strategy, to teach relevant and effective communication skills that will resolve the situations that challenge and stress him.

Teach a communication skill that is relevant to resolving the difficult situation

To develop relevant and effective communication skills as an alternative to more problematic behaviors requires several steps:

1. identify the 'message'
2. identify a means for the individual to communicate the message

3. teach the skill

4. reduce the effectiveness of the problem behavior

5. start to introduce limits and delays

6. making complaints – a useful skill to learn.

Identify the 'message'

As illustrated earlier the behavior may be communicating a message directly or it is possible to identify a communication that would help to resolve the situations in which the problematic behaviors arise. This understanding will be based upon experience with the individual and observations of when the behavior does and does not occur. Sometimes a behavior will involve more than one message – the same behavior may be a way of saying 'Hello', 'Leave me alone' or 'Get me out of here', depending upon the circumstances. It is important at this stage to identify all the messages that the behavior conveys. It can be really hard to know why a behavior is occurring and we may be tempted to guess or assume that it must be 'communicative'. At this stage it would be better to focus on those behaviors and situations that we are sure have a communication element and where we feel confident that we know what the message is.

Identify a means for the individual to communicate the message

The means needs to be something that is feasible for the individual to use. If a person has never been known to speak then setting out to teach a speech skill would not be a wise starting point. It would be better to start with something that is closer to how the person currently communicates (making a gesture or a sign perhaps) or that is within her current understanding. For example, pictures might work for the person who does not yet use them for communication but who is interested in pictures and can identify some already. The common options for communication include:

- speech

- sign

- picture exchange

- gesture

- simple augmentative device (such as a button operated 'speaker' that delivers one or two voice messages)

- complex augmentative device (such as a multiple-choice message board or full keyboard)

- concrete objects.

Applying these ideas to the opening examples suggests:

> Giving a single button communicator to Martin which plays the recorded message 'Let's go'.

> Using a picture exchange for Arnold with a popcorn picture on the cupboard to signify that popcorn is available and which he hands over in exchange for popcorn.

> Providing a concrete object for Simon (part of his twiddler) that was available at 'free play' and that he could hand over for the whole object.

> Teaching Sara to say 'Chase me' when she wants to play.

> Putting a 'break' card on Carl's desk that he hands over when he wants a break.

> Teaching Catherine to say 'Help me' when the computer crashes.

> Teaching Junior to say 'Hug me' when he is getting stressed and anxious.

Having identified the message and a plausible medium, the next step is to teach the skill.

Teach the skill

This will mean identifying the situations and signs when the skill is needed.

> When Martin or Junior show signs of agitation that is when we prompt use of the skill (when we press the button/use the words).

> When Carl is scheduled for work and is starting to resist we prompt him to hand over the break card.

Sometimes it may be possible to artificially increase the number of times that the skill is practiced.

> We only give Arnold a small amount of popcorn when he asks and encourage him to ask again when he finishes.

> We only chase Sara for a little bit and then prompt her to ask again.

> We change the password to access the computer so that there are now more occasions when Catherine will need help.

Most (not all) people learn though repeated tries, so that the more often we practice the quicker the skill will be learnt and the easier it will become for us to use the skill. The skill will become more 'fluent', less energy intensive. In this learning phase it is important that using the skill always leads to a successful outcome.

> Martin always gets to leave.
>
> Arnold always gets popcorn.
>
> Simon always gets the twiddler.
>
> Sara always gets chased.
>
> Carl always gets left alone.
>
> Catherine always gets help.
>
> Junior always gets a hug.

In the real world, of course, you do not always get what you want but at the training stage the competent communication skill must be very effective because it is competing with a behavior that is already effective and well practiced. If it is to replace the behavior the communication skill must be easy to use and effective – hence repeated tries and constant success.

Reduce the effectiveness of the problematic behavior

As we teach the new skill we need to look for ways of making the current (problematic) behavior less effective. We may be able to not reinforce the behavior at all or we may be able to limit the reinforcement achieved.

> When Martin becomes upset we try to calm him and keep him safe without leaving the situation.
>
> When Junior becomes upset we try to calm him and keep him safe without holding him and applying pressure.
>
> When Carl starts to injure himself we work to keep him safe but stick with our demand – we do not back off until at least a small part of the task is done.
>
> We never produce popcorn after Arnold hits someone.
>
> We develop a drill for keeping Sara in sight and eventually getting her back without actually chasing her.
>
> We focus on protecting the computer when Catherine gets mad at it.

Only rarely can we ignore a behavior altogether. If we understand exactly what the person gets from the behavior then we can usually design a way of responding that keeps the person and others safe without delivering the main response that reinforces the behavior. However, this only works well if it goes on alongside the teaching of an acceptable way of getting access to what is important to the individual.

Start to introduce limits and delays

In the real world we do not always get what we want, even if we ask nicely. It is therefore important to work on tolerance for delay once the communication skill is being used consistently.

> Arnold can only ask for popcorn at the times indicated on his visual schedule and if he asks outside those times he will be told 'later' and shown on the schedule.
>
> Carl has to do just a little bit of work before he gets the break.
>
> Sara only gets to play chase in certain places or at certain times and outside those times and places she is told when/where the next game can occur.
>
> Catherine has to wait just a few seconds before help arrives, as in the real world there will often be a delay between seeking help and getting it.

We start with just small limits and delays and gradually build up until we are at the point which is going to be sustainable for the individual's situation.

Making complaints – a useful skill to learn

We all get upset when things that we are expecting do not work out – when a trip, appointment or class is cancelled, when the car breaks down, when people let us down, when there are unexpected changes in our schedule. In some of these situations we have every right to complain – what happened was not fair or appropriate or was a clear violation of a 'contract'.

People with autism are often let down in these ways. Something expected that does not happen is a common trigger for behavioral outbursts. Sometimes this is just part of life. However, sometimes these frustrations reflect the failures of services to deliver the supports that they are paid to deliver. In some circumstances therefore it is reasonable to think about teaching people the more complex social skills of making a complaint. It does not immediately relieve frustration but it does give the individual something else to do when bad news is received.

Making complaints is not a discrete skill with the immediate or short-term outcomes described above. It would be difficult to see how to teach it to some people. The exact skill set would depend upon the situation – making a complaint to Mum or Dad is different to making a complaint to the school, a television network or a bus company. It will need to be combined with the teaching of other skills. In the short term people have to learn the skills of self-calming rather than melting down behaviorally. But they do need to learn that there is more that they can do. The skill set is likely to involve speech (assertiveness) and writing, depending upon the circumstances. Teaching methods are likely to involve coaching and role play. Although this can be quite complex it is a skill set that could help mitigate the ups and downs of life that tend to trigger behavioral incidents.

One useful way of working on this in family settings is to have regular family meetings which can be a forum for giving news, making plans, offering suggestions and making complaints. Special notebooks and forms can be used to help the child with autism articulate his thoughts and coaching can be given during the meetings. Meetings can be videoed to further enhance the skill learning. This would not suit every family and the child with autism needs to have a certain level of formal communication skills (speech, sign or writing). However, if established as a routine, it can be a powerful vehicle for teaching assertiveness and listening skills, both important long-term contributors to effective social functioning.

Teaching communicative alternatives is easier to describe than to do – it is hard work and takes a lot of time and effort as well as a clear understanding of why the behavior is occurring. Still, it is one of the best-validated interventions for effecting longlasting change in seriously problematic behaviors.

Additional interventions for the communication 'I don't want to do that'

Asking people to stop what they are currently doing and do something that we suggest is a very common trigger for behavioral outbursts. We have considered above how to help the person communicate his preference in a more acceptable way – for example, to ask for a break or to say 'No'. There can be a number of other factors that contribute to making requests or demands such a flashpoint, however, and each of these has practical implications for what we do. These factors will now be discussed in turn.

Issues of control

Some people are very driven by the theme of control – they need to feel in control of all that they do and of the world around them and they dislike greatly being told what to do and having things decided for them. Such people may even reject or refuse something that they really like just because someone else offers it to them – they need to choose for themselves. This is a human personality type and some people with autism are like this. There are also theoretical grounds for believing that this trait may be much more common amongst people with autism. The terrifying chaos of the world around them may lead them towards using control as a means of reducing anxiety. The difficulties with social thinking make it hard for them to see any good reason for compromising with other people.

One way of addressing this issue is to present demands or requests as choices. Instead of asking someone to complete a task directly we offer choices:

> Shall we put on pants or socks?
>
> Do you want to do the math worksheet or some reading?
>
> Shall we vacuum or do the laundry?

The choices can be presented verbally and visually (holding up the materials, laying out pictures). The individual gets some sense of control and we retain our control because we determine the choices. It is important to limit the number of choices (two or three is best to start with). Some individuals find making choices itself a difficult thing and will need work on this specific skill before the approach can be used in flashpoint situations.

Demands – the end of the world as we know it

When another person intrudes into your personal space and suggests doing something this can raise additional problems for people with autism. If a person with autism has her attention very focused on what she is doing already, then it can be hard for her to unhook that attention and shift to something else – in fact, it's not just hard, it may feel very uncomfortable. Even if attention can be shifted, it can be hard for her to grasp what is being asked, how long it will go on for, when it will be possible to get back to the things that are important. That kind of thinking presents a real challenge for many people with autism so it is not surprising that demands might trigger a strong, negative emotional reaction.

These issues can be addressed in four ways.

- *Work repeatedly on 'first this, then that' sequences* – here we work to help the individual understand that what we are asking has an end point and to see that something he prefers doing follows the task suggested. We expand the information field available to him and inject motivation because the second activity, which is consequent on completing the first, will be something he enjoys very much. We can present the sequence verbally and visually (pictures or the tasks themselves). Sequence is conveyed by a set order (left to right or top to bottom). The approach can be used not just in the most challenging situations, but in as many situations as possible which involve the person actively participating in tasks. It becomes a ritual. All demands are presented in this format so that, over time, the individual becomes able to sustain more than one item as the focus of attention.

- *Work repeatedly on 'first A, then B, then C' sequences (behavioral momentum)* – this is a variation on the sequencing just described, but this time using a three-step approach. As before, the sequence can be presented verbally and visually. The most important difference is that the most difficult or unacceptable demand is placed in the middle, between two tasks in which the person usually participates willingly. Developing this as a ritual will help, so that it is not just used when we are going to present something that the person finds unpleasant.

- *Use timers and other clues to indicate when a task is finished* – it may be hard for the person with autism to grasp that the work that we are asking her to do will only go on for a short period of time. It may feel to the individual that she is heading for a life sentence of doing art, cutting carrots, doing math or cleaning tables. Thus, trying to make clear how much has to be done is one way of enabling the person to get involved. If the task is time based (it needs to be done for so many minutes) then using a timer can help. Initially the time is set very short and the task finishes as soon as the bell/buzzer sounds or the light flashes. Once the 'game' is understood the time can be gradually increased. Not only does this improve the information available to the person it also reduces the amount of social interaction and confrontation around tasks. The end point of other tasks can be marked more visually – only cleaning up to the tape line on the floor, only cutting carrots until the cup is filled. Again, we start with asking very little so that the task is quickly over and then gradually build up.

- *Increase the reinforcement for cooperating with tasks* – many of the things that we ask people with autism to do are for what we believe to be their own good. From the perspective of the person himself the tasks may at best be meaningless or at worst aversive. It is therefore important for us to be clear that there is some identifiable longer-term gain for the individual in participating. If so then one way of making participation easier is to use a very powerful short-term reward for completing the task or activity (this is an example of the 'first this, then that sequence' described above). The reward may be an edible of some kind, access to a highly preferred activity (such as a favorite video game), stickers, money – whatever truly will motivate the individual to work. The reinforcer must follow immediately after the task or during the task as each step is completed. Access to the reward should be possible only through the specific task – if the person can have the favorite foods, preferred games, stickers or money anyway then this will reduce the power of the reward to influence behavior on the task(s) that trigger outbursts.

Martin was still not toilet trained at the age of 12…and this did not bother him one bit. It sure bothered everyone else and would certainly impact his quality of life as he grew older. He did not like being asked to go to the bathroom and often had tantrums when this was suggested. His family decided to keep his favorite candies just for bathroom trips. He would get one just for going in initially, then for standing for a time set on a timer which was gradually increased and then only when he used the toilet.

There can be objections to the use of these kinds of external incentives, yet it is a perfectly normal part of everyone else's life (most people would not keep going to work if they did not get paid). There is no reason why people with autism should not access the same kinds of motivational supports that everyone else relies on when they are being asked to do something which has no intrinsic meaning or pay-off from their point of view.

I want to be alone

As we have discussed in earlier chapters it is a great challenge for many people with autism to engage in and sustain relationships with others. There is a tendency to slip away from social engagement and become lost in an isolated, personal world. In this world you are following another agenda, listening to a different drummer, and the intrusions of the outside world will be experienced as highly aversive. This issue comes up many times in the book and is described in detail in Chapter 11. Relationship building can be a focus at any time but it is particularly important if we see that the person's resistance to a task or tasks that we suggest is not just about those tasks but is part of a much broader picture of social disengagement. In this case we will need to work on relationship building. If we feel that the individual has become socially disengaged, it is very important that we take steps towards rebuilding our social engagement with the individual. The key areas to work on are described on pp.157–9 in Chapter 11, 'Loss of social connectedness'.

Summary

The problem addressed

- behaviors that arise when the person has an urgent want or need and the behavior is a means of persuading others to do something that solves the problem

- behaviors that arise when a person is upset and if they could communicate a relevant message the upset could be relieved.

Approaches described

- making desired items or inputs readily available
- being aware of the signs of upset and stepping in to bring relief. The plans are based on knowing:
  - the signs of upset
  - the sorts of issues that commonly upset the individual
  - approaches that are effective in calming and settling the individual
- teaching a communication skill that is relevant to resolving the difficult situation:
  - identify the 'message'

- o identify a means for the individual to communicate the message
  - o teach the skill
  - o making the problematic behavior less effective than the new communication skill
  - o start to introduce limits and delays
- teaching people how to complain about 'poor service'.

Additional interventions for the communication 'I don't want to do that':

- issues of control:
  - o present demands or requests as choices
- demands – the end of the world as we know it:
  - o work repeatedly on 'first this, then that' sequences
  - o work repeatedly on 'first A, then B, then C' sequences (behavioral momentum)
  - o use timers and other clues to indicate when a task is finished
  - o increase the reinforcement for cooperating with tasks
- I want to be alone:
  - o work on relationship building.

Ideas to think more about

Write down here any ideas taken from this chapter that you think might help your child.

Chapter 7

I Don't Want You to Say 'No'

Making demands on each other can lead to confrontation. In the last chapter we looked at situations where problematic behavior was triggered when we asked the person with autism to do something and he in effect said 'No'. In this chapter we look at the situations where the person with autism asks us to do something and we say 'No' or where the person is already doing something and we say it must stop. Denying requests and setting limits are common flashpoints for behavior.

> Ellen was a self-starter and was always interested in learning new things for herself. She decided to learn to cook but after she had blown up one microwave her mother decided that she could not be allowed to do this on her own. Whenever she tried to stop Ellen from cooking Ellen would protest loudly and start biting her arm and hitting her head with her fists and her knees.

> Trevor was a bit of a food hound and would often approach his parents, signing 'please', meaning he wanted food. Sometimes it was OK for him to have food but not always. Whenever he was told 'No' he would slap, push and bite either his parents or whoever was nearby.

> Mark was quite happy to shop at the supermarket but wanted to go as soon as all the items were in the cart. If there was a line at the checkout and he was told that he could not go yet he would become upset and pull the hair of other people in the line.

> Gary loved music and music players. At his day program he would find the music players and want to take them home with him at the end of the day. When he was told he could not do that he would throw the

equipment to the ground, start breaking other things and lash out at anyone who tried to stop him.

Barry loved McDonald's and would always want to go whenever he drove past one of their branches. His parents planned their driving routes very carefully to avoid McDonald's if they were not going there. Inevitably there were slip-ups. They would drive past a McDonald's and have to break the bad news that they were not going in. Barry did not take this well and would usually attack whoever was driving the car.

Nobody likes to hear the word 'No'. Try Exercise 7.1.

Exercise 7.1 Suck it up?

Think of specific situations (more than one) that you have experienced when you have really wanted something and have been denied it. List those situations.

- What did you feel?

- How strong were those feelings?

- What thoughts went through your mind?

- What things did you do?

As we look at our own experience described in Exercise 7.1 we can begin to understand why these situations are so challenging for people with autism. The feelings evoked tend to be strong and sudden and we may have to work to manage those feelings. We may sometimes fail and lose our tempers and behave badly. We try to understand why we are being denied. We think of ways round the situation (ways we might persuade the person, other people we can go to, how we might take revenge!). Indeed, we may often find ways of getting what we want and beating the 'No'. As we spell out all these steps we see how people with autism are often stripped of the resources that we deploy in these situations. They may not be able to process the reasons given and switch from the topic to think of something else. They may not be able to think of a way round the person who is saying 'No' or of other people they could ask. They may not notice how upset they are getting and may not know what to do with the strong feelings evoked. If they do lose their tempers they are likely to end up with a behavior plan, psychotropic drug treatment or both.

In the real world nobody really takes 'No' for an answer but we do learn a number of ways of managing these conflicts. However, they always remain fraught encounters especially when the person asking feels very strongly about the issue – it is important from her point of view. It is irrelevant how important it might seem to other people. It is the personal investment and felt experience that is important. Indeed, the real surprise is how often people with autism cope with denial given how few resources they seem to have for such coping. As often in this book, we take time out to learn as much as we can from the individual about what works for her and what does not by doing Exercise 7.2.

If Exercise 7.2 has not solved the problem then the rest of the chapter offers ideas for making these transactions more manageable.

Ways of avoiding the situation

In some situations it may be possible and desirable to avoid getting to the point where a denial is needed.

Say 'Yes'

It is important to reflect on the limits that we are setting. Sometimes we get drawn into denials because we are concerned about power and control. Sometimes concerns about power and control are legitimate (see Chapter 10). But

Exercise 7.2 Coping with denials and limits

List below everyday situations involving denials and limits. List the ones where the individual often copes well, the ones that often lead to a meltdown and the ones that can go either way. Review these lists and identify what it is that enables the individual to cope well in these situations.

Denials/limits often coped well with	*Denials/limits that often trigger behavior*	*Denials/limits that can go either way*

Summarize your thoughts about what factors contribute to a denial/limit being successfully coped with.

sometimes they are not and we find ourselves fighting battles for no very good reason. We should only be denying things if there are significant costs to the person or others incurred by us saying 'Yes'.

Inform when 'Yes' is a possibility

Sometimes when we say 'No' we mean 'Not now, not ever'. At other times we mean 'Not now but later'. Explaining when the person can have what she wants will sometimes avoid the situation escalating. This can be done in words but often will be done better with 'props' such as visual schedules and timers.

> Ellen had a cooking activity scheduled every day. When she went into the kitchen outside of the scheduled time her mum or dad would take her over to her schedule to show her when cooking would take place. They made it even easier for her by having big 'Open' and 'Closed' signs posted outside the kitchen to let her know in another way when cooking would take place.

> Trevor had scheduled snacks and did show some understanding of a visual schedule, so could be shown when snacks would happen. This worked better in school situations where there was more structure anyway. Home was not so rigid about food and the family was happy for Trevor to eat but not all the time. So they used a timer – when the bell rang Trevor could ask for food and was given it. If he asked before the bell rang he would be shown the timer but not given food. Initially the time intervals were set to be short and then gradually extended as Trevor learned the 'game'.

If something is being asked for which is not scheduled, we can show that we understand its importance by going over to the schedule and adding it. If this is not possible it can help to write down what has been asked for on a post-it note and put it on the fridge or a 'To do' list. It is very important that we show we understand how important this is to the other person and that we are looking for the opportunity to say 'Yes'. This can help to reduce the intensity of the response to the immediate denial.

Be proactive – avoid the need to say 'No'

In some situations it is possible to plan things so that we do not get to the point where the person asks for something that we then deny.

> Mark was given a specific supermarket visual schedule. This assigned to him activities (items for him to collect) and when he had completed this

part of the schedule the next step was for him to put on his personal music player. The schedule also included standing in line before going back to the car. By setting Mark up with an activity that distracted him before he had to stand in line, the situation of Mark asking to go to the car, being denied and then having a meltdown was avoided. He was not so bothered about going to the car because he was absorbed in his music.

Gary had his own music player and musical instruments. They were packed into a box and taken to and from his day program. At the end of the day Gary was given his box and asked to choose something to take with him before he left the program. This avoided him taking things that did not belong to him (Gary had no clear sense of private property or personal ownership...he was a true hippy!!) and then being denied these things, thus triggering a major confrontation.

Even Barry's situation was made a little easier by use of a visual schedule and distracting activities. The schedule did help him understand if/when he was going to McDonald's. This was made more powerful by placing the icons representing his destination on any car journey on the back of the front car seats so that he had in front of him throughout the journey information about where he was going. Specific distracting activities were also developed for car journeys (string was a real favorite for him). He still noticed any McDonald's that he passed and still sometimes had meltdowns but they were far fewer and it was a lot easier to refocus him to where he was going and to keep him more settled because he had something else to do during the journey.

It is not always possible to avoid situations where we say 'No'. We have also to consider how we present the bad news as well.

Ways of presenting the situation

'No' is bad news. There is no way of concealing that. However, there may be ways of presenting the bad news that make it a more manageable experience for the individual.

Limit the limits

It is extremely important that limits are set. 'No' must mean 'No' on some occasions; however, we can find ourselves saying 'No' to everything or too many things (see above). We need to learn to say 'Yes' more often. There are also some people who are hypersensitive to denials so that any denial triggers a very violent reaction. We need for these people to identify a very small number of things that we will deny consistently.

This latter dynamic is a troubling one and often part of the broader issue discussed in Chapter 10. At this point we focus on limiting the limits and that will mean saying 'Yes' to things now that later we will want to say 'No' to. We prioritize a small number of denials and, when we have worked out a good way of managing these conflicts, we start gradually to increase the number of limits we set until we have the boundaries and limits that are acceptable in our family context (this is a family decision not a professional decision – it is about the values of an individual family not about the limits that other people think should be set).

Introduce a 'third party' to limit setting

At many points in the book I stress the value of putting information into visual formats. It can be very helpful to people with autism to have their schedule laid out visually. It can also be very helpful to write or picture out rules for specific social situations and post these rules (for example, the house rules for the family). The advantages have been presented in terms of better enabling people with autism to access the information. However, there are additional advantages when it comes to denials and limit setting. If our message is not a straight out 'No' but 'Let's check your schedule/the house rules' this not only alters what we say but the whole body language of the encounter. We do not stand face to face we move away to 'check', our eye contact is not exclusively on the individual but moves between the individual and the schedule/rules. The authority in the situation ceases to be personal; it is not me arbitrarily denying you but the rules or schedule that are 'responsible'. The message is still fundamentally 'No' but the delivery is altered dramatically.

> When Ellen went towards the kitchen she was redirected to check her schedule and the check decided whether or not it was time for cooking. It was still difficult for Ellen to cope with not getting what she wanted but the level and intensity of the confrontation was much reduced.

This tip takes us into a fuller consideration of the specific skills involved in limit setting or denying. The extent of the confrontation triggered can be significantly influenced by how a limit is set.

Use a skilled approach to setting limits

As always it is important to learn from the individual and Exercise 7.2 will have helped to identify some of the specific approaches that help the individual cope successfully with limit-setting encounters. There are also some more general points about these kinds of encounters that often help to reduce the level of confrontation that occurs.

- *Keep a firm, even voice tone – stay calm* – given that the encounter is going to be upsetting it is important for us not to escalate emotions by becoming angry or irritated. If we become personally confrontational (the limit is already confrontational) then it is likely that person's emotions will escalate out of control and the problematic behaviors will emerge.

- *Show sympathy for the other person's distress* – through our words and body language we should try to show the individual that we know that this is upsetting and we are sorry that it is so uncomfortable (even though we are going to stick to what we said). We acknowledge that the issue is an important one for the person – she feels strongly about what she wants. We mentioned earlier that writing down what she wants and posting it to help us remember can be an additional way of showing respect.

- *Avoid the word 'No' as far as possible* – the word itself can sometimes be the trigger – denials may be manageable but the word 'No' is the red rag to the bull. We should look for ways of phrasing denials that reduce reliance on the word 'No' itself. For example 'The schedule says that now we need to be…', 'I am not able to do that right now', 'The rules are…'.

- *Switch the focus to what is needed now (redirect)* – part of the problem for the individual is that she cannot switch her mind from the desired object or activity – it is still there reverberating around, adding to the frustration. One good way of moving a situation on is not to keep repeating the denial but to focus on what the person needs to do now. It will be even better if we can offer choices so that a sense of control is returned to the person – 'Your choices now are… What will you choose?' This message can be delivered verbally, with icons/pictures or with real objects (for example, offering Gary a flute or a maraca from his music maker collection).

- *In some cases, challenge the person by offering acting out as a choice* – this
  is a riskier approach and should only be used with those people
  with whom we can successfully communicate about the value
  of behaviors – about how some behaviors are smart/cool/adult/
  appropriate and others are dumb/nerdy/childish/inappropriate.
  If this is part of our ongoing relationship with someone then,
  once we have set the limit, we can offer choices which include
  acting out: 'Your choices now are to fall to the floor and do your
  kid's tantrum number or to be smart and go work on your computer
  until…'. This has to be used carefully but, psychologically, can be
  an effective way of undermining the power of the aggressive/
  destructive/self-injurious behaviors that are triggered in these
  confrontations. It moves us away from being anxious to avoid
  these behaviors: this is a hidden dynamic which sometimes is
  driving them. The behaviors give the person a great sense of
  power because we get so upset when they occur (see Chapter 10
  for a more detailed discussion of power dynamics). Taking this
  approach makes it clear that we are fine either way, the individual
  must choose for herself and take the responsibility, and we will
  deal with whatever comes our way. Of course, in our heart of
  hearts we are anxious but we have to recognize that our worries
  may actually be fueling/energizing the behaviors and we must
  not to let ourselves be controlled or intimidated in this kind of a
  way. Responding in this way requires considerable skill – it is
  important not to make the challenge a threat ('Go ahead, see what
  happens') or to make it a sarcastic sneer. We have to be genuinely
  behind the message that 'you have control over your own
  behavior and you can choose how to respond right now – it is
  your choice not mine'.

If these ideas are very different to how we normally communicate denials/
limits then it will be helpful to develop a detailed script for the situations
which we encounter on an everyday basis. We should write down the things
we will try to say and how we will try to say them. We should rehearse them
many times over in our minds so that when the real situation arises it will be a
lot easier for us to remember and use our 'new' approach.

At this point we will have done the best that we can do and it is down to
the individual how she responds. How we then respond to her reaction can
also make a difference to what goes on in future encounters. It is to this area we
turn next.

Ways of responding to the other person's reaction

Celebrate if 'No' is tolerated without triggering damaging behaviors

Exercise 7.1 (p.97) has reminded us how difficult it is for any of us to hear 'No' and to cope with denial. If the person copes successfully with a denial (no aggression/self-injury/property damage) then this should be cause for celebration. We need to convey to the person in whatever way we can that we really respect what she achieved – this may be in words, signs, gestures, touches, looks, the offering of a 'treat'. It is important to reinforce successful coping, by which we mean getting upset but not losing behavioral control. Being upset is OK, it is natural. Hurting others, hurting yourself, breaking things, that is the problem. If the individual manages not to act out then that is a great achievement and should be celebrated as such.

Respond in a minimalist fashion if behaviors are triggered

We can present denials in a very skilled fashion but it remains a denial and that fact will sometimes trigger incidents. It is important not to escalate along with the person with autism. We need to keep our cool as best we can, do what is needed to keep everyone safe, see the person through the crisis and get them moved on to something else (see Chapter 3).

Some of the ways suggested for working through denials and limits require that the individual possess certain competences. If these competences are not available then we will need to develop and strengthen them outside of the confrontational situations so that they can be used to good effect in these situations.

Developing background skills and competences

Work on choice making

One of the problems for people with autism is that their minds can be single tracked and they may find it hard to switch from topic to topic – it may be hard for Ellen to get cooking out of her mind, for Trevor to get food, Mark to get car, Gary to get music players and Barry to get the big yellow arches out of their minds. Part of coping with denial is being able to move on and switch topic. Thus, working on choice making more generally will help the individual move his mind between topics. We can look for all the ways that we can give extra practice on choice making so that switching fluency can be enhanced. Working on choice making is best done visually with the items or representative icons simultaneously present and a limited number of choices. We can start with two and only add more when we are sure that the person is fully competent at choosing between two options. If holding more than one thing in your mind and switching fluency are improved then it is easier to move the person on from confrontational situations using the approach of 'your choices now are...'.

Work on 'first this, then that'

Sometimes (as in Mark's case) we are saying that he can have what he wants (get to the car) but only after something else has happened (wait in line, check items, pay money). Although a lot of younger people with autism are exposed to visual schedules and the like, not all of them really grasp what they mean and there are many adults who have not had the benefit of this exposure at all. Thus a number of people may benefit from more specific training using icons or pictures that work on just a two- or three-step sequence where the last item is a reward/preferred activity of some kind. This starts with looking at the times in the day when the person accesses rewards or preferred activities and working with as many of those as feasible using the two-step 'first this, then that' approach. This will mean using the two icons, probably going left to right, cueing the first behavior with the icon, posting the icon away when the activity is completed taking the second icon and having the person exchange it for the reward/preferred activity. This is done in as wide a variety of everyday situations as possible (for example, first dress then breakfast, first tidy equipment then cartoons, first exercise then drink) until the person is fluent in working this kind of sequence which can then be introduced into those denials that are essentially about delays rather than absolute denials. Working on this specific topic also helps to develop the more general capacity to hold more than one thing at a time in one's mind and switch easily between the items. This underlying capacity is critical to being able to move on from situations and let go a current focus.

Work on relationship building

As ever, our capacity to negotiate more difficult social transactions is going to be greater if we are already engaged in a wide range of successful social transactions. It is going to be harder if we cannot do things together – hang out together – in general. If we feel that the individual has lost his sense of social connectedness, it is important that we focus on relationship-building activities. Key areas to work on in order to rebuild our personal engagement with the individual are described on pp.157–9 in Chapter 11, 'Loss of social connectedness'. If we can make progress on these it will make it easier to manage the more confrontational situations.

Summary

The problem addressed

Behaviors can be triggered by telling the individual that he cannot have/do something (either at all or just for right now). This may happen when he asks for it (denial) or we may want to stop something that he is already doing (limit setting).

Approaches described

- ways of avoiding the situation:
  - say 'Yes'
  - inform when 'Yes' is a possibility
- ways of presenting the situation:
  - limit the limits
  - introduce a 'third party' to limit setting
  - use a skilled approach to setting limits
    - keep a firm, even voice tone – stay calm
    - show sympathy for the other person's distress
    - avoid the word 'No' as far as possible
    - switch the focus to what is needed now (redirect)
    - in some cases challenge the person by offering acting out as a choice
- ways of responding to the other person's reaction
  - celebrate if 'No' is tolerated without triggering damaging behaviors
  - respond in minimalist fashion if behaviors are triggered
- developing background skills and competences:
  - work on choice making
  - work on 'first this then that'
  - work on relationship building.

Ideas to think more about

Write down here any ideas taken from this chapter that you think might help your child.

Chapter 8

I Love It When…

The previous two chapters have focused upon behaviors that are about persuading others to do things. The present chapter looks at behaviors that are more like hobbies, passions or entertainments. The behaviors themselves generate an outcome which is very rewarding for the individual but may be less than exciting for others.

> Damon was a whiz at dismantling electrical items – it took him no time at all to remove plugs, take apart phones, faxes, radios and videos. His favorite trip out was to go to the hardware store to look at tools that he could use for his dismantling. He just loved doing this…for the rest of the family of course this behavior was a considerable challenge.

> Anwar might have been a weaver…but he wasn't. He tore fabric into long strips which he arranged very neatly. This brought him great interest and not a little peace. For his family it meant a huge difficulty in keeping bedding, curtains and clothing.

> James had a severe visual impairment and when not in a structured activity he would poke his eye. He seemed to get a real buzz out of this although it was increasing the damage to his vision and led to regular infections in the eye.

> Clark knew exactly what to do to upset each of the other children in his special class. If not watched closely he would go round to each of them and set them off, sitting back to watch the fireworks. This made people very angry, especially as he was 'more intelligent' than the other children and 'should know better'; but he was really just a practical joker and he loved all the action.

> Sylvia loved water and bubbles…and spit…she seemed to be able to produce large amounts of spit and nothing gave her greater pleasure than to spread it around all over the place. From one point of view she was quite artistic, as well as being quite autistic.

To have such a hobby or passion is a great strength. It means that you rarely get bored and always have something to do. However, the above examples illustrate some of the costs that these hobbies can create and the importance of reducing these costs. In many cases this will involve setting limits so it may be useful to read this chapter in conjunction with Chapter 7.

Find a 'safe haven'

Given that these behaviors are a hobby it is important to think about whether we can provide an outlet for them that will not cause negative social consequences. An outlet is a way of allowing the person to indulge his passion but in a carefully defined and limited way. Outlets can be direct or indirect.

Direct outlets

The outlet is likely to be defined in three ways.

1. *Materials* – for example, electrical items and tools for Damon, fabric samples for Anwar, messy play things for Sylvia.
2. *Place* – a work bench for Damon, personal hobby boxes stored in a set place for Anwar and Sylvia.
3. *Time* – when the materials will be available and accessible or when people will be available to talk about a favorite topic.

The principle here is that if we can provide an outlet that is carefully defined and that allows the individual uninterrupted access to his hobby then it makes it easier to interrupt or limit the behavior at other times. Making this happen requires careful and detailed planning. We need to plan when, where and with what the person can indulge himself and how we will disrupt or prevent the behavior at other times.

> Damon had his own work bench and tools and was kept supplied with old electrical equipment. He had free access to his bench when he was at home and there was nothing else structured for him to do. As long as he worked at his bench he was not interrupted and other family members showed interest in his work. If he tried to dismantle anything that was not

on his bench or tried to take items from around the house to his bench he was interrupted immediately and redirected firmly to his bench.

Anwar had a hobby box that was kept filled with the kinds of cloth items that he preferred for tearing. This was always kept in the same place and was available to Anwar when there was nothing else structured for him to do. He was left in peace as long as he worked with his hobby box. If he attempted to tear other items he was interrupted and redirected. However, because supervision was sometimes difficult certain favorite targets (trousers and duvet covers) were adapted to be harder to tear – they were made up specially from sailcloth. Once the discrimination was established and Anwar worked only with his hobby box it proved possible to go back to regular trousers and duvet covers.

Sylvia had a designated water play area at home. There was a bowl with water in it, a smooth table top and a bubble machine. As long as she played there she was left in peace unless there was some other structured activity for her. All around the house there were cloths. As soon as Sylvia began to spit and smear outside of her water play area the surface and her hands were immediately wiped and Sylvia was redirected to her area.

So our planning focuses on two areas: defining an acceptable outlet and disrupting the behavior at other times. Disrupting may mean physically disrupting the behavior – stopping Damon, Anwar, James and Sylvia when they try to do their thing. It may mean disrupting just the effect of the behavior – only having toughened materials readily accessible for Anwar so that he cannot easily rip them, wiping up Sylvia's spit the minute it comes out of her mouth so that she does not get the chance to play with it. The key principle is to reduce the likelihood and amount of reinforcement for engaging in the behavior outside of the 'safe haven'. We present the individual with a choice – dismantle the household equipment, tear up the curtains, spit and smear all over the place and get a lot of social intrusion and aggravation; or work at the bench, hobby box, play area and indulge yourself without being interrupted. With a consistent approach the behavior gradually comes to focus more on the outlet. At first the outlet needs to be readily and frequently available but over time the availability can be reduced to 'hobby times' or 'free times' and understanding of this can be enhanced with the use of visual schedules which tell the person when she will be able to indulge herself.

This form of discrimination training requires detailed planning and a lot of consistency. It is hard work. However, it is usually quite successful. It does require constant monitoring as the basic desire does not go away – relax and you'll find your phone dismantled, your duvet neatly shredded and your surfaces covered in spit! The person with the passion can usually outwit the person who does not share that desire and it is important to be able to see the funny side of that. In soccer terms, by setting up safe havens we are playing for the draw rather than a win.

Indirect outlets

It is sometimes not safe or desirable to provide a direct outlet for the hobby. It is not OK to damage your eye…ever. It is not OK to torment other people…ever. Our approach then is to look for something that comes close to providing the same result as the hobby behavior but that is safer and more desirable. In James's case we look for sensory activities that produce interesting visual or touch stimuli, such as flashing lights or vibratory massage. In Clark's case we look for some other skill that would get a reaction from others (for example, doing magic tricks, telling jokes or doing comedy routines). This is a more challenging approach. It requires something that comes close to the chosen hobby in terms of effect but is not the 'real thing'. It is likely to require a period of training in order to develop the skill to the point that the person can readily achieve a result from engaging in the behavior.

If those steps are achieved then we move on to doing the same things as we do for the direct outlets. We start with structuring a lot of access and then gradually reduce it until the hobby takes a more normal place in the overall pattern of life. We make sure that we help the individual understand when hobby time will come around.

A NOTE ON THE VALUE OF HOBBIES

These behaviors can drive other people mad and create considerable costs. However, they can also be of tremendous value to the individual. As already mentioned they give the person something to do when there is not a structured activity available and this is very important at home, where it is simply not possible to structure life in the way that we can at school (for example). These behaviors can also be the source of a valued social place. The obsession with dinosaurs, deep space or sports statistics can make you the best person to have on the quiz team and cause others to choose you. The interests may also lead towards employment if a job can be found that fits with the passion. Thus, although we try to limit them and although we may not always see the value in the particular hobby, it is important to remember that there are advantages to these behaviors. These advantages probably outweigh the disadvantages.

Having said that, it is important not to allow the individual with autism to become trapped into having just one interest. She may always have a dominant interest but interests do change over time and it is important that we promote such change so that the individual truly does have a choice about what to do and the hobby does not become an addiction.

Expand interests

It is often hard to predict which new activities will prove 'winners'. All humans tend to resist change and are often unwilling to try new things. However, if we can be inspired, cajoled, persuaded or pressured enough into trying something, especially if we can try it more than once, then we can discover new joys and interests. The hobbies of people with autism often seem to come out of nowhere and can also change very suddenly. Close examination shows these interests almost always come from some kind of experience – either an experience that the person has generated for themselves (from spit weaving to finding something on the Internet); or an experience that he has been persuaded into by others. Sometimes the uptake is immediate, sometimes delayed. What is for sure is that we do people with autism no favors just by settling for what they already do or like. We need to keep expanding their experiences so that over time they can more truly make informed choices about their preferences. This is as true for adults as it is for children. Sometimes this is hard to do – asking someone if he wants/wants to try something that he knows nothing about will almost always elicit the answer 'No'. So there will be times when we do not make things a matter of choice. This does not mean that we 'force' someone but that we use the resources of persuasion at our disposal to get them to access an experience or activity. This can be a difficult moral decision, especially with adults. We will have to justify why we want to bypass choice and have good reasons for believing that the person will benefit, that it is 'in his best interests'. However, it is equally important to understand how autism can paint someone into a corner. It can lead individuals to unnecessarily restrict their experiences and may unnecessarily impair the quality of their lives. Even those whom we regard as highly intelligent can lack the critical capacity of conceiving possibilities and remain dominated by present actualities and past experiences. This means that they lack the capacity for informed choice unless they have the direct experience. In these cases, persuading someone to try the experience can be justifiable and is part of what we do to help people avoid being dominated by a single interest or hobby. Working with the behaviors that are the focus of this chapter means respecting people's current interests but also continuing to challenge them to develop new interests.

New interests become particularly important when faced with the situation in which we are justified in taking steps to discourage a present hobby.

Work towards discouragement

Clark's behavior is one where some attempt at direct discouragement would be justified. Samantha illustrates this even more clearly.

> Samantha hit the sides of her head hard with her hands. She did not speak and had learned very few skills over the 30 years of her life. Recently the self-injury had begun to escalate. Intensive assessment indicated that the behavior did not serve any social function (it was not about getting out of tasks or uncomfortable situations, not about getting people involved with her). The most likely causes were pain or some kind of self-stimulation. Exhaustive medical tests could find no physical basis for Samantha's behavior, which left the possibility of self-stimulation. Given Samantha's learning history it was clear that teaching alternative activity skills, while part of the approach, would be a very long-term effort. In the meantime wounds were opening up on her head and it was increasingly difficult to protect them and to get them to heal. In the circumstances it seemed justifiable to target some work towards actively discouraging head hitting.

In the past active discouragement often meant some kind of aversive stimulus (pain shock, water spray, white noise) applied each time Samantha went to hit her head. Such techniques are controversial and arouse strong feelings. While their use has declined it has not disappeared altogether and there are those that argue that they are justifiable in extreme cases. This book is a broad-based, general book about the behavioral issues that families of children with autism have to deal with. It is about approaches that can be readily incorporated into family life. This is therefore not the place to get into a topic of bitter controversy that involves interventions that can be quite technical in nature. It is the place, however, for pointing out that there are plenty of less controversial approaches to helping Samantha (aversives are not 'the only way'). There is a range of reward-based approaches which give the person something positive for not doing the behavior in question. These are combined with finding a less direct outlet for the motivation that is driving the behavior (see above) and sometimes more direct attempts at reduction.

Reducing by reward

This idea is essentially making the person a positive offer that he cannot refuse. It means finding a powerful incentive which can only be accessed by one of two things.

- Doing anything other than the behavior of concern.

Samantha could be doing anything other than hitting her head to get small amounts of chocolate pudding.

Clark could be doing anything other than winding the other kids up to earn points towards computer time.

- Doing something specific that interferes with the behavior of concern.

Samantha could earn small amounts of chocolate pudding for holding on to bags or pushing a cart.

Clark could earn points for sitting in his place and doing word search puzzles during unstructured time.

These approaches usually start just at certain times of the day, specific 'sessions' when we work to bring the behavior down. Once we have shown that we can reduce the behavior we expand to other times. Sessions are usually signaled.

We put a special bracelet on Samantha to signal the start of the reward program.

Clark has a visual schedule which tells him when it is choice (unstructured) time.

The criterion for reward is worked out based upon how often the behavior is currently occurring.

Samantha hits her head on average every five seconds so that we start by rewarding her for every two seconds she keeps her hands away from her head.

Clark tended to tease the other children every few minutes in unstructured time so he gets points for every minute he does not tease.

As the behavior reduces we extend the amount of time that has to pass before the reward is earned. If the behavior occurs it is blocked or interrupted and only when the situation is settled again do we go back to the reward plan. The behavior therefore delays reward – the less the behavior occurs the more often rewards occur, the more the behavior occurs the less often rewards occur.

This approach to reduction certainly takes time and effort. It is not a long-term solution. Clark needs to learn his constructive 'audience reaction' skills and Samantha has to learn, for example, a self-massage and communication skill (ask for 'head rub') if long-term progress is to be made. However, these other interventions take time to become effective and positive-based reductions, such as those described above, provide a shorter-term 'breathing space', when the behavior is too dangerous to be allowed to continue for very long.

Reward…and disruption

Although the emphasis is placed upon the positive reinforcement aspect of these interventions, part of the approach is to disrupt the behavior when it does occur – to block Samantha from impacting her head, quickly to interrupt and redirect Clark when he goes to tease. This disruption is quite likely to cause distress and be unpleasant for the individual, even though the intervention is judged to be in the person's best interests. Being positive about behavior support does not necessarily mean that distress never occurs.

From passion to purgatory – when hobbies become compulsions

We have so far focused upon activities which bring some kind of pleasure or satisfaction to the individual even though they may create disruption for others. There are occasions when these very same activities fail to bring satisfaction; indeed, they cause more and more distress. That same bit of video that the person likes to watch over and over, he still watches over and over but somehow it seems not to be quite right, the repetition becomes more and more 'driven', creating more and more agitation…yet he cannot seem to stop. The same flappy or building materials are still sought out but again they do not seem to be quite right and can't be made quite right…but the person keeps at it getting more and more wound up and unhappy. This is when a hobby becomes something more like a compulsion. It differs from classic obsessive-compulsive difficulties because in these the act that we label compulsive brings some kind of (short-term) relief from anxiety. For the person with autism in this mode, on the other hand, nothing that she does with her hobby seems to bring relief or satisfaction. Yet she cannot let it go. She is stuck repeating over and over, never getting to a place of comfort. It is more like torture now.

This kind of switch from hobby to torture almost always occurs in the context of a more generalized loss of personal well-being. It is not just that the hobby no longer brings satisfaction but that *nothing* brings satisfaction. Old intolerances return, nothing seems to be enjoyed. This more generalized loss of well-being is a very significant contributor to some of the most serious behaviors that we are faced with. It is a topic addressed in Chapter 12 where the ways of promoting and retrieving personal well-being are detailed. However, while we are working on the more general sense of well-being it may be the kindest thing to block access altogether to the 'instrument of torture' – to hide away the videos, building materials and the collector's cards, to refuse to discuss dinosaurs and the concept of time, to block access to the cartoon channels. It may not be feasible to do this altogether and we may only be able to reduce exposure. But it is certainly kind to try to relieve what was once a source of comfort but is now adding to the sense of discomfort. When well-being returns then we can try going back to how things were, to see if the Lego, cartoons and the like can once again function as a useful hobby; or maybe a return to well-being will bring an openness to the development of new interests.

Well-being is not the only background factor involved in these private passions. Sometimes an individual will become increasingly involved in them as part of a general drift to social disengagement. He slips away from relating to others and focuses more and more on self-generated stimulation. If this is part of the picture then we will need to focus on rebuilding social engagement as part of our approach to limiting the engagement in private passions. Chapter 11, 'Loss of social connectedness' looks at rebuilding personal engagement with the individual (pp.157–9), and it may be vitally important that we look at this.

Summary

The problem addressed

Behaviors that are like hobbies, that are reinforcing in and of themselves but create problems either because they damage property, cause physical harm, create social upset or there is conflict when attempts are made to limit them.

Approaches described

- finding safe havens:
  - finding an acceptable direct outlet for the behavior but with limits on the times, places and materials when the hobby can be pursued
  - finding an indirect outlet for the behavior which does not deliver the same experience as the current behavior but delivers something close to that experience
  - disrupting the behavior outside of the situations we have defined as 'acceptable'

- expanding interests to find replacements for current hobbies

- in some circumstances, working to discourage the behaviors using positive reward strategies and disruption when the behaviors occur

- removing access altogether or as much as possible when the hobby has become a torment for the individual

- working on relationship building to empower our efforts at teaching, accessing new experiences, redirection, distraction and limit setting.

Ideas to think more about

Write down here any ideas taken from this chapter that you think might help your child.

Chapter 9

I Feel Terrible

Many behaviors occur when the individual is in some kind of negative state – anxious, upset, miserable, hurting. In more positive mode the individual copes with the situations that trigger behavior. However, once he is suffering discomfort then other motivations take over (for example, I want to be left alone, I want to be held) or he can no longer inhibit impulses and loses control of his behavior.

David had a lot of problems with his bowels (constipation) and after three days without a movement he would every so often and with no immediate trigger start screaming and slapping his head.

Katrina had very mixed feelings about going to school and on school days would be difficult to wake, would often start asking repeatedly 'Am I going to school today?' and sometimes would escalate to biting herself and smashing her knee into her face.

Sam would sometimes arrive at his day program in an obviously agitated state and this would often escalate to him pushing, hitting and trying to bite others.

Between four and six in the afternoon was a reliably difficult time for Mike – he would moan a lot, would be unwilling to cooperate with any task and would often have major tantrums when he would throw and break things.

Nolan was in many ways quite an easy-going guy but there were some days when he was 'hell on wheels' – nothing would please him, he was very oppositional and verbally abusive and sometimes he would get physical with other people.

Negative mood and physical discomfort are obvious influences over behavior. We all know from personal experience how we can behave when we ourselves are upset, irritable or in pain. We often make this observation about other people – that they are 'in a mood' and that explains why they are behaving badly. We know that many of the more challenging behaviors shown by people identified on the autistic spectrum are accompanied by clear signs of negative emotionality and that we can often predict incidents based upon observations of emotional state. Yet somehow it is only in the last few years that this notion of mood has begun to be taken seriously in its own right – that it might be something that we target for change rather than targeting the behavior directly. This is all the more bizarre as there is a huge literature in general psychology that looks at mood and has researched techniques for influencing mood.

It is important to be clear that this chapter is not about the more general-ized and pervasive negative physical and emotional states. The broader based issue of general well-being is considered in Chapter 12. This chapter is not about the deeper causes of distress such as loss or trauma; these issues are also considered in Chapter 12. This chapter is about the more transient mood or physical states that all humans go through, sometimes in response to events (traffic, lines at the supermarket, headaches, an argument, coming back to work after a vacation, indigestion, lack of sleep) sometimes in relation to time of day (early morning, mid afternoon). These states pass of their own accord but they may pass more quickly if we target specific 'mood management' activities. That is what the chapter is about – doing things that may produce a short-term change in mood or physical state that in turn will reduce the likeli-hood of the behaviors that tend to occur in this state.

As often in this book we will consider first what we can learn from the individual. Exercise 9.1 will help to focus on what we know already that may help us to solve the problem that we are concerned about.

Building on this knowledge of the individual which we have explored in Exercise 9.1, we will now review some of the ways in which we can help people experience a greater degree of comfort and more frequent positive moods.

Relieve common causes

There are a number of things that will tend to cause bad moods and discom-fort and that should be the target of intervention.

Exercise 9.1 Mean...moody...? Magnificent!

Fill out the following for your child:

Signs of comfort/positive mood

Signs of discomfort/negative mood

Things that promote comfort/positive mood

Things that create discomfort/negative mood

Things that can turn discomfort/negative mood into comfort/positive mood

What ideas does this suggest for reducing the likelihood of the behavior that is of concern?

Social conflicts

People can be in a bad mood because they have been involved in some kind of conflict with other people – they have been denied something that they want, they have been bullied or teased, they have been pressured to do things that they find difficult or do not understand. If a bad mood is caused by a social situation and it is unreasonable to ask the individual to cope with it, then obviously we should do what we can to relieve that situation (part of which may be teaching the individual better skills at being assertive or responding to bullies). Mood will also be impacted by conflicts going on around the individual, even if he is not directly involved in them. He will be impacted when he is exposed directly to others arguing and by the general atmosphere in an unhappy home/class/work situation (see below). We need to look for ways of reducing all kinds of conflicts, whether the individual is involved directly or not.

Social atmosphere

Linked to the conflicts is the less observable phenomenon of social atmosphere. Emotions pass between us quite readily. If we are around people who are angry, tense, hostile, we readily pick up those feelings. People with autistic spectrum disorders are especially vulnerable to this as they have more difficulty in distinguishing between their own and other people's feelings and tend to be more open and sponge-like to other people's feelings. They may not be good at reading the feelings of other people at a cognitive level but, like all human beings, they pick up those feelings and are more vulnerable precisely because they cannot analyze them and know where they came from. Thus sometimes the distress that we attribute to the person identified as autistic is more truly the distress of those around them. Our focus needs to be on relieving the tensions at home/in the classroom/in the place of work, not just on lightening the mood of the individual. It would be a personal impression that anger and fear are the two most readily 'transmissible' negative emotions. The positive side of this is that people may be very open to the more positive and inspirational motivations that others can bring to them.

Reinforcement drop

Some people are very sensitive to a sudden drop in the amount of positive reinforcement that they are experiencing. When the fun stops it is only natural to feel a bit down. However, some people seem to go far beyond that. When the fun stops they turn very nasty, becoming angry and hostile rather than a bit down. Thus the ending of something positive is a good predictor of a sudden mood shift. If your son or daughter is sensitive in this way then one way into this is to try to effect a more gradual reduction in positive reinforcement – to stage him/her out more gradually from highly reinforcing situations. In other words, save some of the good stuff for after the main event.

> Every Friday night Jason would go out to dinner with his parents. He loved it and behaved well in the restaurant but on the way home in the car would often attack his parents. By developing some special fun car toys, shifting to having dessert at home and putting on a favorite video after dessert, the situation in the car improved (icons were used to help Jason understand what was happening and to see that the end of the meal was not the end of the positive world).

Pain

Clearly proper treatment of physical problems is required. David's self-injury virtually disappeared once an effective way was found of keeping his bowels moving on a regular basis. However, dealing with pain is not always this straightforward. It is hard to know sometimes if a person has a headache, sinus pain, joint pain, muscle pain. For those without speech there is an obvious problem, but even those with speech may not be good at reporting on internal states. If there is any evidence that pain issues are involved in negative states then discussion with the individual's physician should be undertaken to weigh up the pros and cons of using pain-relieving medication even if we are not 100 per cent certain that there is a pain issue. This might include the use of antacids or reflux relievers, given the frequency of gastrointestinal problems for people with autism.

Lack of sleep

Sleep issues for people with autism are varied and deserve much more consideration than can be given here. Some people with autism take very little sleep as a general rule; but this is usually a problem for those who live with them not for the individuals themselves. Some generally sleep well but have nights when they take no sleep at all. This does not cause immediate problems for the individual but may do so if the phase continues beyond a few days. Others may have difficulty sleeping through the night, wake often and seem to get tired and irritable in the day. There is no specific amount of sleep that is good for you (humans do not necessarily need 'eight hours'). It is a matter of individual differences. Frequently disturbed sleep (including days without sleep), however, seems to have a greater impact on functioning in the day. If the individual seems to be getting poor sleep, below are some of the things that may help.

- Be rigid about getting-up time and, more flexible about going-to-bed time. You cannot force someone to sleep but you can wake them up and the sleep system seems to organize itself more easily around waking-up time.

- Develop a fixed, calming routine (see p.126 for elements to put into such a routine) for going to bed that is initiated when the person shows signs of tiredness.

- Do not worry too much about naps in the middle of the day (if the social situation permits them) but try not to let them go beyond 60–90 minutes or take place soon after getting up or after about 5–6pm in the evening.

- Use a 'minimalist' response to night waking and try to settle the person back as quickly as possible, using elements of the original settling ritual rather than some new/novel intervention.

- A specific sleep medication may help to (re)establish a routine but there is less likely to be merit in the long-term use of sleep medications.

If none of the above helps, consider consultations with a neurologist (to assess for night-time seizures) or a psychiatrist (to assess for depression or bipolar disorder or other mental health issues that may impact sleep). If these interventions do not help consider seeking a referral to a sleep disorder clinic.

Develop a mood management plan

Variations in mood during the day or over a week are perfectly normal. We all do a lot, often without realizing it, to manage our own moods. Many people with autism find it difficult to monitor their own mood states, to understand the causes for their discomforts and to know what to do about the feelings they experience. Once again they are deprived of the resources which come to others quite naturally – most of us never specifically learned 'mood management'. People with autism are much more dependent upon others both to offer assistance with mood and to develop the understanding and skills needed to self-manage discomfort. For the purposes of this section it is assumed that if we know that there is a specific issue causing the distress we try to sort the problem out. This section focuses on situations where we either have no idea what the problem is and no way of finding out or where the problem cannot be resolved immediately.

We look first at the direct assistance that we can offer – how others can intervene to turn around a negative mood and avoid it developing into a behavioral outburst.

Identify clearly the signs of negative mood

The first step is to identify generally what emotions we see the person going through, what are the observable signs of the various emotions and which particular emotions are associated with the behaviors of concern (see Exercise 9.1). If the individual cannot report at all on her internal state then this stage is about assembling our observations. If the person can report then we can combine information from her report as well as our own observations. The point of this stage is to be as clear as possible about the signs, especially the early signs, of negative mood or discomfort. This is important in helping our own focus but is especially important if we will be involving other people outside the family who may not be fully aware of some of the less obvious signs of difficult mood. Below are examples of the kinds of list that one may end up with.

- Weaving head, making low moaning sound.
- Jumping and squealing.
- Pacing rapidly, waving arms, vocalizing loudly.
- Pushing people and/or furniture, biting arm.

- Head down, shoulders hunched, shuffling walk.
- Talking about a 'negative' topic (why a certain TV show is no longer available).
- Being unable to focus on assigned tasks.

- Complaining that other people are interfering/causing trouble and starting to argue with them.
- Shouting and using cuss words directed at these others.
- Threatening to hit/kill people, blow the building up.
- Leaving seat and going to hit/kick others.

Identify mood altering interventions

The second step is to identify the kinds of interventions that might help to turn around a mood. Exercise 9.1 will have generated ideas and there is also a large research literature to draw upon that indicate the kinds of things that can have an effect in turning a negative mood into a positive one in the short-term. These activities bring arousal level to a more optimal stage (not too much, not too little) and relieve negativity. They include:

- about ten minutes' brisk exercise (to be distinguished from more extended periods of exercise that build fitness)

- repetitive activities

- quiet time

- food

- music

- laughter

- massage (especially deeper-pressure approaches like shiatsu).

One might add aroma to this list, although I am aware of less research on this topic. What should also be noted very carefully is that none of the known mood shifters involve speech and language. Talking about problems may be good for finding solution, but will not necessarily make you feel better in the short-term; and the focus here is on short-term change.

From these options it is necessary to identify the ones that work for the particular individual – that produce a more optimal level of arousal and relieve negativity. It is important to choose elements that both work and can be easily applied in the real world situation when a negative mood is apparent, either on a preventative basis (see section later in this chapter on transition rituals) or in reaction to clear signs of negative mood. Using the vignettes at the beginning of the chapter we can look at how this might work out in practice.

> Before Katrina got up in the morning classical music was put on. She was woken gently and when she asked about school she was directed to her weekly calendar which color coded school/non-school days. As she got washed and dressed opportunities were taken to provide some hand and arm massage. The breakfast things were laid out so that the options could be seen and speech was kept to a minimum. After breakfast Katrina took a short walk up and down her street before getting into the car and heading off for school.

When Sam arrived at his day program in an agitated state he was encouraged to one of the smaller, quiet rooms and his Lego box was offered. A staff member stayed with Sam, working with him and listening but saying very little. Sam was offered a shoulder massage and when he seemed in a calmer state Sam was encouraged to rejoin his group and join in the planning of what to do for the day.

When Nolan was starting to get angry and wound up he was reminded that he was acting angry and prompted to look at his cue card for what to do when angry. The card outlined a number of 'good choices' for him to make when angry – these included:

- ask for help
- take three deep breaths
- ask to take a break and go for a ten-minute walk
- listen to some favorite music on your personal player while walking.

A number of points need to be made about mood targeted interventions. These are short-term 'fixes' – they do not deal with more severe and pervasive mood problems like depression although they can play a role in breaking up such a mood on a daily basis. These interventions will interfere with pre-planned activities but the point is that if escalation continues these activities will be disrupted anyway and to a more severe degree. Getting someone settled raises the likelihood that the activities will be successful even though it may temporarily take away time and resources. It makes no sense to plough on with an activity in the face of someone getting increasingly upset and out of control – no-one will gain from that. Finally, there is the fear that somehow we might end up reinforcing bad behavior. The point of mood interventions is that they are planned to occur before any behaviors occur. We do not wait until someone is attacking others, injuring themselves or breaking the place up. We respond to clear signs that the person is in a negative state but not actually behaving badly. Once problematic behavior has started it will be responded to in the agreed ways (see Chapter 3). Once an incident is over and dealt with, if the person still seems agitated or unhappy it would be wise to consider mood-shifting work before the person gets back into the activities of the day.

Develop a formal mood management plan

If a written plan would be helpful then we can adapt the format first described in Chapter 6 (p.85) as shown in Exercise 9.2. (p.128).

Exercise 9.2 Format for mood management plan

This identifies the signs, what we think they mean, and the interventions that we will use to try to turn the upset and discomfort around and put the individual more at ease and in a happier frame of mind.

When...	We think it means...	And we will...

Develop transition rituals

Moods can come and go in relation to events and experiences. Sometimes it seems as though moods can have a life of their own – we do not always know why we are in a good mood or a bad mood. In this sense moods are very individual – to the person and to the life she is leading. However, there are a number of more universal situations where mood has a tendency to negativity. These are commonly the major transition points in a day. Some we might term 'biorhythmic': starting the day, coming out of sleep into wakefulness and gearing up for the day's activities; the mid–late afternoon 'slump' when many people feel tired, irritable and find it hard to focus or get on with things. We could add to this list going to sleep, not because in and of itself it is a fragile time but because it is very easily disrupted by high levels of arousal and energy or agitation, stress and worry.

The second transition type is not so noticeable for many people (though it is there) but is very clearly an issue for many of the people that we identify as autistic. This is the impact of transitions between activities in the day – when we have to stop what we are doing and shift to doing something else. Transitions have a cognitive dimension (what am I doing now, what am I doing next). But they also have an emotional dimension – they tend to produce an arousal 'spike' and we develop (often unconsciously) rituals which help to smooth the process of transition. If we think carefully about what we do:

- when we get to work or come home from work
- at the end of a meeting before going on to the next activity
- when we have finished the household chores and we are going on to do something else

we will find buried in there 'little things' that we often do that do not seem to have any real practical purpose. We could easily go from doing one thing to doing another without doing those things, but somehow those things are there. They are there to help smooth the emotional dimension of attention switching.

It is not surprising that transitions (biorhythm based and activity based) are often 'flashpoints' for behavior and a good transition ritual will help to reduce the likelihood of such behavior. It is an important preventative measure. A morning transition ritual was illustrated earlier in this chapter for Katrina. Mike, whom we described at the beginning of the chapter, clearly also needs a transition ritual for the late afternoon. We incorporate into these major transitions attention to the following.

- *Sensory ambience* – lighting level, noise level, amount of speech, type of music, presence of aroma.

- *Activity* – a repetitive activity, brisk exercise, a laughter-inducing video or game, massage or another relaxer such as a bath.

- *Sustenance* – food and drink.

We use the elements known to impact mood and energy with the aim of generating both positive feelings and a moderate degree of arousal – not too much, not too little. Rituals around sleep differ in that we want elements that bring positive feelings but also encourage lowered rates of arousal as a prelude to sleep. Thus we might avoid including in a night ritual brisk exercise, high energy music, laughter or stimulating food or drinks, items that we might well incorporate into other transition rituals.

Activity transition rituals of necessity need to be briefer. They might include:

- warning signals a few minutes ahead of the change (spoken, some other kind of auditory cue such as tone, a bell, a few musical notes or a visual cue such as a specific colored card). Warning signals and their accompanying time period allow arousal to be spread out over time and heads off the large surge that can occur when stopping and refocusing is pushed through too quickly

- a specific transition activity with a strong repetitive element (for example interacting with the visual schedule – move icons around, tick off the completed activity on a checklist)

- a brief physical 'diffuser' (brief massage, some stretches, a few deep breaths).

One of the schools that I have had the privilege of working with over many years incorporated these elements at the beginning and end of each period both to reduce disruption during transitions and to optimize attention to the learning tasks at hand.

Mood management and transition rituals incorporate the same elements. Mood management is a way of responding to an observable situation – someone is in a negative emotional state and we need to do something to turn that around. Transition rituals are a longer-term fixed part of life that occur anyway. We do not go to a transition ritual when we see a transition going badly, we do it anyway. It is a long-term preventative approach, part of the lifestyle that can play a role in promoting positive well-being, optimizing learning and reducing the likelihood of those behaviors strongly associated with negative mood states.

Both the approaches described so far involve 'outsiders' (parents, teachers, support workers) taking action to affect the mood state of the person with autism. That person in many cases will not understand why these things are done – he may not understand the feelings he has, he may not understand the links between his activities and experiences and his feelings. He is in that sense the passive recipient of the good works of others. These days there is much emphasis upon independence and this encourages us to think in terms of self-regulation. Could the individual learn to register and understand her feelings and initiate activities that would impact those feelings? There are plenty of materials on teaching people to read other people's feelings, some on getting people to read their own feelings and some on teaching people emotional management skills, usually some version of relaxation training. What is missing from many of the materials on self-regulation is a developmental perspective on the topic. Managing our own feelings emerges after the early years of life when others manage them for us. Out of the experience of receiving comfort, grows the ability to recognize feelings and manage them. Children who do not receive comfort from others, either because it is not offered or because it is not effective, find it a lot harder to learn self-regulation, are easily overwhelmed by their feelings and are prone to difficulties with impulse control. It is not certain that the experience of comfort from others is necessary or sufficient for the development of self-regulation, but it is certainly a significant contributor.

This point is emphasized because it is sometimes not recognized as important for people with autism that they should experience emotional comfort from others. It is a vital part of the human relationships that we work to forge, even with older people, that we try to bring comfort when the person is in distress. We must be careful not to be blinded to this by injunctions to 'ignore bad behavior', 'avoid spoiling', 'act age appropriately', 'reinforce independence', 'use tough love' or notions like 'he's autistic, he doesn't need that kind of stuff'. We cannot always do it – sometimes it is hard to reach out to people and make things better. Our well-intentioned efforts may only make things worse and in the end the person may best be left to get out of the distress in his own time and own way. However, we should not be dissuaded from trying and we should not rationalize our incompetence as being a special technique for people with autism. Let us bring comfort if we can because out of that may grow the capacity for self comfort, something which is most certainly a valuable goal.

Thus part of developing self-regulation is, paradoxically, developing our capacity to bring comfort. People with autism often have to be helped specifically to learn things that come naturally to others (even as others have to learn specifically what may come naturally to the person with autism). So there are specific things that we can do to develop those competences we call 'self-regulation', that work alongside our efforts to be a source of comfort.

Build self-regulation

This breaks down into a number of specific activities.

Develop awareness of emotions

This can be done by:

- drawing attention to our own feelings (exaggerating their expression, labeling them with words or an icon)

- feeding back to the person what he is feeling when we are absolutely sure what the feeling is (commenting with words or showing an icon for that feeling as it is actually happening, or reviewing videos we have taken)

- discussing feelings we see illustrated on the TV programs that the person enjoys

- using Social Stories™ to illustrate feelings in specific social situations

- using structured teaching materials to teach identification of illustrated feelings

- involving the person in drama activities to learn to portray different feelings.

Once the basic feelings (I would suggest 'happy' and 'angry' as the best starting points) can be identified in others and in the self it is important to enhance the feedback to include the events that create feelings. We need to start sketching out 'why' feelings occur. This kind of causal understanding is very hard for many people identified as autistic – they are often at a complete loss to understand why they have the feelings they do. This applies as much to people with well-developed speech as to others. We need to describe the links in words or pictures – whatever medium works best for the individual.

Develop the ability to scale emotional intensity

An important element in self-regulation is recognizing the strength of a feeling – mild negative feelings may not require any action, moderate feelings may need some attention and intense feelings may require an 'emergency response'. For this we will need some kind of visual scale to represent strength of feelings. This can be done in many ways:

- a tachometer (with its red zone)
- a thermometer
- a series of balloons of varying sizes
- a stoplight sequence
- a simple number scale.

The visual scale then needs to be used and taught by integrating into our methods for teaching the identification of emotions:

- drawing attention to our own feelings and rating them on the scale
- feeding back to the person what they are feeling when we are absolutely sure what the feeling is and trying to estimate where on the scale it falls in terms of intensity
- discussing feelings we see illustrated on TV programs the person enjoys and discussing how intense they seem to be
- using Social Stories to illustrate feelings and their intensity in specific social situations
- using structured teaching materials to teach identification of the intensity of illustrated feelings
- involving the person in drama activities to learn to portray different feelings at varying intensities.

Teach emotional management skills

TEACH A NEW SET OF SKILLS

Depending upon the situation the individual might access some specific teaching of a set of emotional management skills. The traditional approach would be relaxation training which focuses on breathing control and muscle tension control. Effective skills might also be taught as part of a broader approach to well-being such as yoga or tai chi. Again, depending upon avail-ability, the individual might work with a massage therapist or aromatherapist to learn some specific techniques of self-massage or how to use aromas.

REVIEW THE CURRENT SKILL SET

Many individuals already have some effective ways of reducing negative feelings – they may have learned to take themselves to a quiet place, learned to play preferred music or 'zone out' with a specific activity. It is important to document these in terms of what they are and how effective they are. Often people have good skills but do not use them in some of the real world situa-tions where they get upset, either because they do not think to or because there are access problems (no quiet place, or they do not have their walkman, juggling kit or bag of twiddlies).

Develop a specific self-control plan

This brings together all the above elements into a plan to cope with specific situations in the real world often associated with negative feelings and behaving badly. The plan details what to do when negative feelings start esca-lating along the scale. Two brief examples from 'work in progress':

> Mark is learning at home to use a modified clock face to scale emotions. When negative emotions start to move to the higher numbers he is learning to first inhale from a favorite piece of cloth which is impregnated with a lavender/chamomile aroma. If the numbers do not come down then the next step is to ask for 'pressure' (self-massage will be taught but is not a skill he possesses right now). If the numbers still do not come down then Mark takes himself off to his room for quiet time.

> Sanjay is learning at school to use a tachometer drawn on to a card to rate his feelings. As things escalate he puts on his headphones (no music). Next he clasps his hands and takes three deep breaths. If the revs are not dropping he asks for a break.

In both these situations the individuals are being coached in real time to use these plans. The plans are written on to a 'notice' posted on the wall for Mark and a small card for Sanjay. The adults are prompting the boys to follow the plan and reducing this prompting so that they shift to true self-regulation. Of course, not everyone can be reached in this way and there are others who could cope with more traditional forms of sessional training with a therapist, including 'homework assignments'. They might have less need for 'on the spot' coaching from a supporter. As with all things, our plans have to be tailored to the individual and the circumstances.

Summary

The problem addressed

Behaviors that occur in the context of negative states, either mood states or physical states. They do not occur or occur much less often outside of these states. The states are the best predictor of incidents rather than the environmental circumstances. The states considered are the more temporary, passing states not more chronic, longlasting states associated with serious medical or mental health problems.

Approaches described

- relieve factors known to contribute to bad mood/negative state:
  - social conflicts
  - social atmosphere
  - reinforcement drop
  - pain
  - lack of sleep
- develop a mood management plan:
  - identify signs of emotions
  - use techniques known to affect mood – about ten minutes' brisk exercise (to be distinguished from more extended periods of exercise that build fitness), repetitive activities, quiet time, food, music, laughter, massage (especially deeper pressure approaches like shiatsu), aroma
- develop transition rituals
- build self-regulation:
  - be an effective source of comfort to the individual
  - develop the individual's awareness of emotions and their causes
  - develop the ability to scale emotional intensity
  - teach emotional management skills
  - develop a specific self-control plan.

Ideas to think more about

Write down here any ideas taken from this chapter that you think might help your child.

Chapter 10

I'm in Charge Here

When people with autism are young they often have no grasp about social boundaries, and consider the world their oyster and other people their servants. They get very upset when limits are set. That is not what this chapter is about. People with autism can have specific passions and intolerances and, when they cannot indulge their passion or are exposed to their intolerances, they become upset and act out. That is not what this chapter is about either. This chapter considers the situation of a person with autism (who has previously learned to understand limits and has built tolerances) starting to set rules for other people and using violence to gain compliance with the rules set.

> Candy would take a dislike to certain words that people used. If someone used a word that she did not like and refused to alter the word she would attack the person. The words that she did not like changed on a regular basis.

> Jack decided that the family dog should not be allowed in the back garden. If the dog were let out he would become very agitated, start to break things in the house and attack anyone who tried to stop him.

> Jared began to insist that no-one should talk at meal times and if anyone talked he would physically attack them.

> Marcus decided that the living room was his room and only his room and anyone else who tried to enter it was attacked and forced out.

This problem may start with a specific rule but then new rules may be added. It usually starts at home but then spreads outside. It usually (but not always) begins in adolescence/early adulthood. It is often accompanied by more generalized and intense feelings of anger and hate. Some will direct their anger and hate at others (for example, anger at their parents for 'making me this way'). Some will direct it at themselves ('I'm no good', 'My brain needs to be fixed', 'I must find a doctor who will take the autism away'). Although there are a lot of negative feelings involved, the individual may also start to show pleasure and excitement at the power that is experienced. This phenomenon can occur at all levels of ability but is most strikingly seen in individuals with good verbal skills and IQs measured above 70. This dynamic builds over time but often with an accelerating course. Some of the individuals may become increasingly preoccupied with internal thoughts and indeed complain of these thoughts taking them over so that they cannot get rid of them. For some new learning will come to a halt and there may even be regression in skills. Although some of this may look like normal adolescence the resemblance is superficial. This is about the direct control of others and the use of violence to achieve that control. It is about a trend of escalation and in some cases it is about a more comprehensive breakdown in personal functioning. The individuals are certainly not in a balanced state of well being and this chapter should be read in conjunction with Chapters 11 and 12.

This is a difficult dynamic to discuss. It is painful for families to admit that they are frightened of their sons or daughters and have ceded control of the house and family life to them. This is made all the more difficult if the individual is functioning well in other environments, even though experience shows that this is often a temporary difference. Others then interpret the situation as being the parents' fault – it is a result of them not being firm enough. This topic has also been made difficult to discuss because there is very little mention of it in the contemporary literature and, indeed, there is almost a denial that people with autism could behave in this way. This neglect or denial is particularly obvious in the literature on Asperger's syndrome/high functioning autism. Yet, when I have described my personal experience of this issue as a clinician on the training courses that I present in the UK and USA I have seen a lot of nodding heads, heard a lot of matching stories and watched some family members breaking down in tears. That is why I have decided to include consideration of this topic because it is so challenging, so painful for the families and so dangerous for the individuals (who in the end may find themselves in secure facilities of one sort or another). While there may be mental health components to this process it fits no single mental health diagnosis. As there has been such a neglect or denial in the literature it means that there is little evidence-based guidance on what is the best way to approach these difficulties.

Hence this chapter should be treated as 'first thoughts' from a clinician. It is a starting point – some of the ideas may be wrong and there is much more to learn about being effective in these situations. However, given the urgency of the practical situations that families find themselves in and the complete absence of useful guidance it seems important to do the best that I can do in order to be of some assistance now and, I hope, to trigger greater interest from the research community in the future.

The interventions discussed range from the general to the highly specific and are presented in no particular order of priority.

Develop a 'like a rock' relationship style – a relationship of psychological strength

When someone is spiraling out of control (even as they take more and more control) it is a very scary thing. It may be physically scary because of the violence to oneself, to others, to property. It is psychologically scary. It generates many anxieties about what will happen to the family and the individual, and generates many sadnesses – 'What has happened to my beautiful boy?' It is very frustrating. It is emotionally overwhelming and threatens us with loss of control.

The one thing that people spiraling out of control do not need are people around them who are spiraling out of control. They need people with strength and resilience – not physical strength, *psychological* strength. They need people who can stand by them, stand up for them and stand up to them. They need people with commitment but a degree of distance (this of all things is hardest for families) – people who are there for them but are not going to be overwhelmed and not going to be rushing around doing everything possible to make it all right for them. They need people with cool determination who will not engage in high expressed emotion.

How do we achieve this style of approach in such fraught situations? It means tapping in to the thought processes that we have around the individual and the behavior and challenging some of those thoughts. These are some of the thoughts that I try to focus on when I am trying to help someone who is in this situation:

I can never make anyone change their behavior but I can do my best to help people change.

People have choices – I can do my best to help people make smart choices but in the end it will be the individual's choice… I cannot make people's choices for them, they have some responsibility, it is not just me

Although the person with whom I am dealing is a smart young person/adult, socially and emotionally he/she often much more like a younger child.

Good control is self-control – I need to say that and show that in my behavior.

This is a long process – I am less concerned about whether we succeed today than about whether we are turning a situation around and establishing a trend to improvement.

No mistake that I make is irretrievable.

I am not the only one going through this and it is not my fault – it is one of the many vulnerabilities related to autism.

It is not that everyone has to think like this. What is being illustrated is the need to develop thinking patterns around these issues that will enable us to sustain our support to the individual and not be overwhelmed by him. Each person may find his own way of thinking that will help but the thought processes are key, so that we can inhibit or turn to productive use the very strong feelings that are evoked.

Within this overall framework of a psychologically strong relationship there are many specific techniques that can be used to develop positive momentum.

Clarify the house rules and post them

House rules are those rules that apply to everyone in the house. It may be possible to engage the individual in the process of deciding on the house rules or it may not. It is important that a small number of basic rules (no more than five) are clarified. For example:

We respect other people's property and do not damage things that belong to others.

When we are angry we use our words or take some quiet time – we keep our hands off other people.

We speak with polite and kind words not hurtful words.

These are rules for family life in general but the individual should also be helped to understand where he may set some rules (for example, in his own room) and be helped to clarify these so that there is a notion of balance of control.

These rules (house and individual's) should be put into visual form (words, icons, pictures) and posted in the house. They should be referred to when limits are being set or behavior challenged. This helps to defuse the personal element in limit setting – it brings in a third party, the 'real' authority, THE RULES! There should be an agreed review system for the rules (for example, at a regular family meeting) so that any complaints about the rules have a clear place where they are dealt with. This stops the process of being drawn into confrontational debates about 'Why?' each time a rule is invoked.

Reference to rules will also be important to cut into discussions that, if left to run their course, often lead to an escalating confrontation. A question about 'Why do I have to go to school' is best dealt with by pointing out that it is the law rather than an extended debate on the intellectual and financial merits of education. The more extended debates are best left for when the person is more stable.

Reframe the behavior

Part of our challenge to the individual is a mental one. It is not just about challenging control over specific issues in the home, it is challenging the individual to think differently about what he is doing. This means finding particular ways of describing inappropriate and appropriate behavior, ways that challenge the person to see his aggressive behaviors as valued less than his self-control behaviors. It is best to start with some idea of the kinds of words that the individual likes/does not like to be said about him. We may know this from our knowledge of the person (he seems very pleased when he is called 'cool', very upset when he is called 'a baby'). We can add to our knowledge with a more structured assessment. Exercise 10.1 (p.142) is one such assessment which helps to find some useful key words to describe behaviors.

Once we have some key words that appear meaningful to the individual, we can use those words as tags or frames for behaviors. The behaviors we want

Exercise 10.1 It's only words...but some mean more than others

You will need paper, pens and post-it notes.

- Sit down with the individual when he is in a good mood – draw or get the person to draw a self-portrait.

- Draw lots of stick people with speech bubbles around the portrait.

- Tell the person that you are going to think about the words other people might say about him and see which one he would like them to say.

- Think of a word, write it on a post-it note, ask if he would like people to say that about him – if so, stick it on the self-portrait; if not stick it on another (blank) sheet.

- Repeat until you have a number of words that the person clearly does and does not want 'stuck' to him – encourage the individual to contribute words.

to build and encourage get tags from the positive list, the ones that we want to discourage get words from the negative list. Thus when we are commenting on behavior we draw from this vocabulary – 'The way you used your words then was really cool/adult/appropriate/strong'; 'I'm sorry you're feeling so weak today/that the terrible two-year-old has shown up/that you're choosing to be inappropriate'. Great care is needed in delivering these messages. They must be delivered in a firm but emotionally neutral way, in line with our preferred relationship style. It is vital to avoid being patronizing, sneering or sarcastic – the emotional tone will certainly be picked up. We can add to this approach by giving written guidance about self-management ('cool'/'smart' things to do when angry). An illustration of this approach was given in Chapter 5 (pp.71–3) although the speed of response in this case was not at all typical. This technique is rarely about a moment of insight and more commonly a long-term way of challenging and seeking to alter the individual's thoughts about her own behavior. It is important for us to realize that people have a frame of reference for viewing things and that if we can insert key social learning ideas into the frame of reference, if we can find 'tags' that are meaningful to the individual then the messages may well be easier to take on board. That also applies to the next point.

Attach key messages to respected sources

Young people do not really want to listen and learn from their parents or stodgy professionals. They may be more prepared to learn if the message comes from a source to which they give credibility – a book, a website, Harry Potter, Spongebob, Tony Hawk, a favorite baseball player. However, sometimes a stodgy professional will do.

> Carol was battling her parents over bedtime and video games. However, Carol was very interested in things medical and very ready to listen to advice from doctors. Thus, when her doctor talked to her about sleep hygiene and gave her some back-up reading materials she became much more willing to accept some of the limits that her parents had been trying to establish.

Real materials may be available or it may be possible to draw the individual into a more imaginary discussion ('What would Tony Hawk do if his mother wanted to watch something on television that he did not want to watch?').

Again the approach is to fit our key social messages into a frame of reference that enables the individual to both understand and accept those messages and be more motivated to work towards improvement.

Maintain and extend cooperation

It is very important to be looking for ways of maintaining and extending any of the situations where the person does something that we ask (chores, homework, helping out in other ways). We can negotiate what these are but we should be very committed to having at least a minimal level of cooperation. Although in this kind of unstable state the individual will not be able to cope with a lot of demands, it is not wise to withdraw all demands. We cannot force people to do things but we must feel very strongly about making some demands and be committed to doing all that we can do to see that the cooperation is achieved. It is reasonable and right for us to do that and safer for the individual in the long run.

Use reinforcement

Experience suggests that in this state people remain accessible to the effects of positive reinforcement. It is vital that successful coping and cooperation are positively reinforced. However, delivering such reinforcement can be a considerable challenge.

Candy would get overwhelmed if she was praised and this was quite likely to provoke an incident.

Jack would get very upset if he was offered a 'deal' of a reward for his cooperation in some area – he would accuse his family of bribing him, get very angry and sometimes become aggressive.

We can consider three options for delivering reinforcement.

1. *A formal, spelled-out system* – not everyone is like Jack and some people remain accessible to having a contract that spells out what is expected and some kind of chart that records when they succeed. The system may use points, tokens or money and the rules need to be clear about what you do to earn, and when you receive the money or trade the points and tokens either for money or another agreed reinforcer. A common mistake with these kinds of systems is to set the criteria too high (so that the individual ends up never getting reinforcers); another is to have too long a delay (the reinforcer is at the end of the week/month). It is a useful rule of thumb to start with a daily system and only extend the time between behavior and reinforcement once it is clear that progress has been achieved by the daily system.

2. *A stealth system* – for those who see a formal system as a challenge to their control and whose behavior is therefore worsened by such a system it is possible to consider a systematic approach but one that is not spelled out in words and charts. It is a system held in the heads of the parents. When key behaviors, such as self-control or cooperation, occur something good follows soon after them, a good thing that never happens unless such behaviors have occurred. The link is never spelled out and questioning can lead to the reminder that we as adults are allowed to…give you money/offer you computer time/offer you a trip to Jack-in-the-Box. That is something we have control over – you have control over whether you accept the offer (this helps to reinforce the lesson that we all have control over things but no-one has control over everything).

3. *An 'in the moment' approach* – a third approach to delivering positive reinforcement for positive behavior is not to have too much of a system at all. There is no planned or automatic link between a positive behavior and a reinforcing event. However, when good things happen we will every so often do/offer something that the person finds reinforcing and we will not make these spontaneous offers without the positive behaviors having happened. We will have

a spontaneous celebration. There will not be a detailed, structured plan and the reinforcer will not be drawn from a prepared list but will be something offered on the spot, that is available immediately and seems like it would be reinforcing to the person. We can spell out the link but we never offer the reinforcer ahead of the behavior as a means of inducement (we do not say 'If you calm yourself down we'll make popcorn'; we do say after you've handled a situation well 'That was fantastic, I'm so pleased, I'm going to make popcorn – want some?'). The trick here is to deliver reinforcement without triggering the control dynamic which can be activated when we offer inducements up front.

Positive reinforcement is always important but is particularly crucial at this time when the person is getting into a lot of confrontations and there is a lot of anger and criticism flying about. It is also crucial because the other component of behavior modification, use of cost consequences, is often ineffective.

Use costs?
People in this state of being are often untouched by costs. Costs will be levied but to no avail. More and more costs will be levied, still to no avail. It may be that the underlying biological mechanism, the motivational system that responds to aversive stimulation, has become deactivated in this kind of state. It may be that the person's power drive is reinforced by making people angry and having them levy costs – the response of levying the cost is reinforcing and this outweighs whatever impact the cost has. Whatever the explanation behavior often remains unaffected by the use of cost consequences.

The second problem with costs is more practical. Costs have to be personally meaningful and they must be levied immediately after every incident of behavior. It is hard to find things that are meaningful and that can be used so swiftly. However, if such an event can be found and the person is impacted by costs then they will play a small role. For example, whenever Candy hit anyone at home all her videos were instantly removed and locked away for 24 hours.

Set (a few) consistent limits
In the situation that we are considering in this chapter setting limits is by definition a problem. It is often the flashpoint for significant aggression/ self-injury/property damage. Inevitably that will make us wary about setting

limits. However, it is part of what we have to do if we are going to turn the situation around – we have to be able to say something is not going to happen and stand by that. Given the dangerousness of these situations it is likely that we are going to focus on just one thing where we will stand firm, as frequent confrontations are too costly for all concerned. This means that we will let some things go, allow the individual control in some areas that may not be ideal but that we will let go for now so that we can use our energies more effectively. We need to be focused, clear, calm but firm. Not too much to ask!! Chapter 7 discusses in more detail ways of setting limits that reduce the confrontational element. The limit(s) that we set will depend very much on the specific situation – the family situation and the exact way in which the power dynamic is being played out. However, limits are an important element in our approach, as we struggle to re-establish some equity and balance in our relationship with the person. Once we have established one boundary we will probably want to move on to others until we have reached a point where there is a reasonable balance of control in the home (again that point will be very much a family decision).

> Candy's family decided that they would not let her control the words other people used but that they would let her take her meals on her own in the kitchen (another rule that she tried to impose).

> Jack's family decided to let the dog out when Jack was not around but did confront him about control over the mail that came into the house (Jack wanted to go through all the mail and only let others have what he decided they should have).

Develop a personal commitment to change

The way that the discussion has gone so far has emphasized battling with the control dynamic using 'external' approaches – attaching messages to credible sources, encouraging cooperation, using positive reinforcement, using costs, setting limits.

However, we want to build the individual's own motivation to change, to bring the person to the point where she sees that there is a problem and wants to do something about it. The 'like a rock' style helps with this – we are remaining neutral but available and emphasizing the notions of personal choice. We do not blame the person for the behavior but we do hold her accountable – how he behaves reflects choices that she is making. We have also discussed cognitive reframing which is again a way of motivating the individual to make better choices about how she behaves. There are a number of other approaches that can help to build and strengthen the individual's own motivation to do better and move on. What now follows draws heavily on the approach known as 'motivational interviewing' which is referenced in the Resources at the back of this book (see Miller and Rollnick 2002). This is not lecturing people about their behavior – no human ever changes his behavior as a result of a lecture or an explanation as to why it is important not to do what he is doing now. Handing someone a plan for change is likewise an ineffective intervention. The process is more subtle and requires listening to the individual drawing him out and bringing him to the point where he wants to change, sees the possibility of change; at this point a plan for change may be effective. The specific ways of building this kind of commitment are: listening for and encouraging talk about the disadvantages of the present situation; listening for and encouraging talk from the individual about the advantages of change, doing things differently; building the confidence to change.

Listening for and encouraging talk about the disadvantages of the present situation

The people with autism on whom this chapter focuses are often very articulate. They may see no problem in what they are doing and/or see it as a problem without possibility of a solution. They can blame themselves or other people deeply, but do not really analyze the situation further.

One step to encourage is to help the person get specific about what is problematic about what they are doing – to detail and write out the disadvantages of behaving in this way but, at the same time, to acknowledge and list what is gained by behaving in this way. Social Stories™ can be used to draw out the specifics of the costs and benefits of current behavior but without the suggestion at the end about doing things differently – the person needs to come to that conclusion for himself, not receive advice from another.

> Part of the work with Candy was to draw out what the problems were with hitting people who did not use the right words but part was also to list what she gained by behaving in this way.

The role of the listener is not to take sides, not to argue for behavior change, but to help the individual analyze the pros and cons of what he is doing now and reach his own decision about the need to change.

Listening for and encouraging talk from the individual about the advantages of change, doing things differently

Again, the people concerned may be very articulate in many ways but do not really see what would be gained by changing. Any talk they may start about change or doing things differently needs to be listened to carefully and encouraged. If the conversation can be developed over time, then listing the advantages and disadvantages of change can bring the person to the point where she is actively seeking to move on. Again, Social Stories may be a way of developing these conversations.

Building the confidence to change

This is woven into the 'like a rock' style. Although the style is low on expressed emotion, part of what we are seeking to convey to the individual is our belief in her and that she can move on…when she chooses to do so. We see and remain optimistic about positive possibilities. We can develop this message by encouraging conversations about problems in the past that the individual has faced and overcome. We can develop it with the use of feedback charts.

> Part of the work with Marcus was to develop a chart which illustrated clearly when he functioned really well. The times of the day when he did well were vividly colored and the chart was designed to show that much of the time Marcus handled himself well. It could be seen at a glance – no conversation was necessary. The chart was for feedback only – it was not part of any reinforcement scheme.

Confidence can also be built by the life book activity described next in this chapter.

If we can develop the individual's personal commitment to change then he will be more ready to take part in whatever plans we have for achieving change. The pace of change will be quicker and the likelihood of a long-term positive outcome will be raised. It may not always be possible and we still have much to learn about how to achieve this for people with autism. However, at some point we do have to learn how to move on from an exclusive reliance on externally driven change. We need to learn how to enable the person to channel her talents and energy away from controlling others and into controlling and developing herself. Psychotherapy will not do it. Behavior modification will not do it. But perhaps there are other ways.

Develop a positive 'My Life' book/journal

This is often a bleak time in the lives of the individuals with autism as well as their families. They hate themselves and hate the world. It is important to rebuild a more balanced view of the individual for the individual. It can be helpful to start assembling a 'Me and My Life' book. This can be a journal for the individual to write in, a place to put in 'credible materials' giving good advice (as above), a place for photos or other representations of being happy and successful, a home for projects such as 'Things I am good/not good at', 'Me in five years' time'. It is part of the process of helping the individual find some light at the end of the tunnel.

These are the approaches that inform my current work with families going through this situation. Future research will help us to sort out which of these are effective and will contribute to the development of new practice ideas. However, as I stressed earlier, this situation is a difficult and potentially dangerous one that has been underplayed in the literature to date. It is a matter of some urgency that the problem is recognized and the work of establishing an effective practice that will move us towards a positive outcome is begun.

Home alone?

A number of additional elements are likely to be part of the work we do. Although there are very serious concerns about the use of psychotropic medications with people identified as on the autistic spectrum, it is quite likely that such medication will have a role to play in helping the person through this most difficult time in her life. It is therefore important to try and access a competent psychiatrist to be part of the team. Many families fight these battles alone and that is something that service provider agencies should be very concerned about. Families with adolescent/adult sons and daughters need just as much access to competent behavioral, emotional and practical support as the families of younger children. Targeted services and a team approach are needed if the likelihood of positive outcomes is to be increased. Such service provision must include a crisis support element, either going into the home or offering brief out of home care. Sometimes situations will develop which cannot be safely managed by the family alone. This element can be relatively small if we can get to the dynamic at an early stage. It has been my experience that this dynamic develops over quite long periods of time (many months) and that the warning signs are relatively easy to spot. A targeted local service would be in a good position to move towards early intervention as opposed to crisis intervention.

This in turn raises the question of outcome – what happens to the young people and their families who get into this situation? There can certainly be sad stories – young people may move to out-of-home care as the crisis unfolds, because the present situation can be handled better there and not because this may be in their overall best interest. Some do find themselves involved legally (in the criminal justice or mental health systems) and end up in secure provision. But it is perfectly clear to me that families can come through this situation. It may take time (one or two years is my general 'rule of thumb') but the situation can move on, a degree of calm can return and then the person may be open to the 'great prize' – a life of his own that works for him.

These days there is much emphasis on intervention in the early years of life. However, it is now clear from basic biological research that the brain remains open to growth and development across most of the life span. This ties in with clinical impressions that for some people with autism, adolescence and adulthood can be times of positive and explosive growth. This is doubly exciting as adult life is in many ways potentially easier to manage than child-hood for people identified as on the autistic spectrum. There is no longer an 'enforced curriculum', there are many more niches to slot into – a wide range of constructive lifestyles that respect the unique talents and gifts of individu-als. We tend to value eccentric adults and pathologize eccentric children. There are also some excellent examples of how services can be constructed that respect and support individuals rather than forcing them to lead the kinds of lives that other people regard as appropriate. The transition to adulthood needs to be viewed with excitement for its possibilities. We need to challenge the approach to resource allocation that favors younger ages and leaves services for adults dramatically underfunded. There is a lot to play for. The dark tunnel does not go on for ever if we can reach in to provide sensitive and effective help. And once people have moved on from the destructive mode described in this chapter, there can be great lives ahead.

Summary

The problem addressed

Behaviors that are about enforcing rules on others by violence and intimida-tion and rejecting all attempts by others to set limits. The behaviors are accompanied by high levels of negative emotions (anxiety and, especially, anger). In some cases the individual's learning stops or regresses and internal thoughts or sensations add to the level of distress.

Approaches described

- developing a distinctive relationship style ('like a rock') – a relationship of psychological strength
- clarifying and posting basic house rules
- reframing behavior
- attaching key messages to respected sources
- maintaining/extending cooperation
- using positive reinforcement:
  - formal systems
  - stealth systems
  - 'in the moment' approaches
- possibly using response costs
- setting (a few) consistent limits
- developing a personal commitment to change:
  - listening for and encouraging talk about the disadvantages of the present situation
  - listening for and encouraging talk about the advantages of change, of doing things differently
  - building the confidence to change
- developing a positive 'My Life' book/journal.

Ideas to think more about

Write down here any ideas taken from this chapter that you think might help your child.

PART 3

Underlying Issues

Part 3 looks at two broader-based contributors that act as 'drivers' for some of the specific themes discussed in Part 2. Chapter 11 looks at loss of social connectedness and Chapter 12 at loss of personal well-being. The chapters describe what these factors are and how they affect behavior, and offer specific suggestions for addressing the needs. There is space at the end of each chapter for writing down ideas generated that seem helpful to the specific issues that a family faces.

Chapter 11

Loss of Social Connectedness

We have illustrated in Part 2 of this book how behavior can be seen as reflecting specific themes. These themes summarize some immediately present environmental or personal circumstances – persuading others to do or not do something right now, what is the noise right now or my mood right now. But sometimes when we look beyond the immediate circumstances we can see broader-based, more pervasive issues which seem to be contributing powerfully to the behaviors of concern. They are not the immediate triggers of incidents but they certainly seem to be involved. In cases where this is apparent, these broader issues need to be addressed alongside the more immediate themes described in earlier chapters.

The first broader issue to be considered is clumsily labeled 'loss of social connectedness'. This refers to the situation where the individual is functioning in several of the following ways:

- spending a lot of time physically away from others

- spending a lot of time mentally away from others, engaged in self-chosen and absorbing, repetitive pursuits

- physically rejecting attempts by others to be close or intrude

- refusing to cooperate with requests to do things

- behaving in these ways even with people who, in the past, were effective at spending time with the person and getting him to cooperate.

The number of people actively involved in the individual's life may also be increasingly few in number.

This way of being represents a change and is in contrast to past times when the person experienced more social engagement. Of course, people with autism, by definition, have problems with accessing and sustaining social engagement. However, social engagement does develop over time and what we are examining here is a loss or decline in what the individual had achieved. It is both a qualitative and a quantitative issue. The individual can no longer engage in the give and take of social life – will not spend time with others, will follow no directions, will accept no limits. When you look at the number of people involved in the life of the individual, you see that there are very few, probably much fewer than in the past.

Why is this a problem? Leaving people to just do what they want to do might seem like respecting a choice. Sadly, it is not the path to happiness and adjustment. This kind of extreme social withdrawal is associated (over time) with increasing signs of distress and escalating behavioral issues. The reasons are hardly surprising.

Human beings do not function well in social isolation, devoid of positive social engagement and attachments. We are biologically wired for interdependence. Isolation undermines physical health (for example, poorer immune functioning), mental health (for example, depression), problem-solving capacities and reality orientation (for example, the tendency to paranoia). It is the greatest cruelty of what we understand about autism. Autism disrupts both the capacities to form relationships and the motivation to do so. Yet people with autism cannot escape the biological imperative of interdependence. They may say that they do not need people and that they do best when alone and, indeed, this is how it feels to some people; but experience indicates that when people are left alone there may be a temporary improvement but this is followed in the long run by a decline into distress and confusion.

People with autism can end up in this effective isolation for a number of reasons. For some it is an active choice. Others may 'slip away' unnoticed. Gradually the siren call of the senses leads them further and further away from social contact and it is only when the extreme point has been reached that others notice. Some may be actively encouraged to withdraw into personal worlds because those who support them follow superficial concepts of 'independence' and 'choice'. This usually happens as people make the transition from school to adult life. Adult services may rightly seek to develop independence and choice, but if this is not carefully thought through it means that anything goes, nothing anyone does will be challenged and any refusal to engage will be accommodated. This can lead some people to spiral rapidly into complete social isolation, followed soon by intense behavioral issues. The final path to social isolation is one of active withdrawal caused by intense feelings of discomfort and distress. The individual feels miserable and hopeless and withdrawal brings some temporary relief. This in turn reinforces the trend to withdrawal until end game is reached when the misery and distress are still present but are now turbocharged by the complete isolation. This last dynamic towards social isolation will be considered further in Chapter 12, which focuses on well-being.

As we consider the things that we can do to retrieve someone from social isolation, we will not really be identifying new techniques. Part of the function of this chapter is to draw attention to a contributor to behaving badly which can easily be overlooked when we focus just on the immediate determinants of incidents. The second function, following from this, is that sometimes in order to effect change in behavior we need to focus not on the incidents but on rebuilding human contact and functioning human relationships – that is the priority which may in and of itself change behavior or make it possible for us to do some of the other things that are needed if behavior is to change (for example, teach new skills). We seek to create a 'listening space'. Many of the interventions described earlier in the book involve teaching, redirecting, building understanding. These cannot take place if the individual is lost in a personal world and is processing no information coming in from other people. Rebuilding social connections is in part a way of making other interventions possible to implement. This point has been emphasized in several chapters. However, being socially engaged brings more benefits than this – social connections bring security, laughter and good health. Other people may be the source of some of our greatest stresses but they are also the solution to these stresses. They are the lifeline. Attending to this lifeline is often a key element in behaviorally focused work.

Rebuilding social connections involves a number of different activities.

Rebuilding our personal engagement with the individual

It is vitally important that we work on ways to become socially engaged and influential again when the individual has fallen off the social cliff. We need to be able to see the value of investing our resources in reestablishing contact and involvement, not just in managing the behavioral issues. The section below describes how we can go about reconnecting with an individual who has become lost to us.

There are three key areas to work on:

1. building tolerance for the presence of another
2. doing activities together
3. following directions.

Building tolerance for the presence of another

Building tolerance is a focus when the person finds social presence so difficult that he tends to move away or push the other person away. It means finding the 'zone of comfort' – the most the person can tolerate in terms of physical closeness, body language (height, movement, eye contact) and noise (speaking, singing, humming for example) from us. We start at the 'outer limits' (this may be, for example, sitting silently on the floor six feet away) and gradually try to move closer, getting to be on the same level and for some noise to be permissible. We want to reach a point where it would be possible for us to do an activity together with the person. Sometimes copying what the person is doing helps to break down the barriers, sometimes showing interest in whatever she does or wherever she looks (you will find these ideas, which are drawn from basic mother–infant interaction research, in the approaches described as 'Floor Time', 'Options' and 'Intensive Interaction'). This kind of work will be done at specific times (most families will not be able to spend long hours doing this) and its aim is to get to the point where we can comfortably do something together.

Doing activities together

Doing activities together may start with working together on an activity that the person themselves already does – we may sit and flap with string, rock gently, play with our spit, line up cars, look through catalogs. Or we may know that there is an activity that we can set up that the person will usually readily participate in – making cookies, rolling marbles, shooting hoops. Again, this work will go on in short sessions until the person's comfort zone allows for us frequently and readily to be able to do certain things together.

We are then in a position to move to a situation where we can take a more directive role and set up activities where the person is following the directions that we give.

Following directions

Tolerance for accepting directions may be built in a number of ways. We may use an activity that we can already do comfortably together and start teaching/encouraging the individual to do more of that activity – to take over our bits of cookie making or doing the dishes. We may introduce an activity that is neutral (that the person neither likes nor dislikes) and encourage him to do that using powerful incentives each time he does part of the task (this takes us much more into direct behavioral shaping and a discrete trials type of approach). We are working towards a point where the individual is willing to do a range of activities that we suggest (and that are not self-chosen) and no longer requires high levels of external reward for doing these things (though she may require some, at the level of – 'Finish this activity and then you can... Homework first then computer time... Load the dishes then dessert').

When we have reached this level of 'social amenability' then it is a lot easier to use interruption and redirection in general – we have a relationship in which there is some listening. It is then a lot easier to do the more specific kinds of interventions described throughout this book. But more than this the individual is now more secure, more socially anchored, less 'lost in space'. More fun can be had!

From the outside in – bringing more people into constructive social engagement with the individual

Here our focus is on increasing the amount and diversity of social input that the individual receives. This can involve a number of activities.

Enhancing our own relationship with the individual

We may want to devote our resources to see if there is anything more that we can do to spend constructive time with our son or daughter. This may mean looking for more activities that we can do together happily or just spending more time together (a major issue in most families).

Supporting natural engagements

People meet each other. Contacts are made. More contact is sought. This happens to people with autism just like it happens to other people. However, if events are just allowed to follow their natural course nothing may come of this. If the individual attends a special class in a designated school, he may travel on a separate school bus and may live further away from the school than anyone else who goes there. Sustaining any connections made will require planning and transportation. Even if the person is going to school or working locally, developing potential contacts will take effort and organization from others as the person with autism may not know how to develop a relationship or even see the point. It is an oft-repeated story that a child with autism will invite a friend over and then completely ignore the friend after the first five minutes. Some planning of the visit to try and sustain contact, some work with the person with autism (see below) and some support to the visitor may help to ensure that the first visit is not the last.

Developing community presence

Going out into the community can often be a fraught experience for many families whose sons or daughters present significant challenges in their behavior. Yet for those who are very isolated even the brief contacts that can arise from being recognized as an individual in your own right have significance. Being known in the coffee shop, the library, the supermarket, the hardware store, the video rental store ensures more frequent and diverse 'social intrusions' and these 'intrusions' (the greetings, the smiles) are delivered positively (unless of course the individual has blotted her copy book by behaving badly in these places!). This kind of presence may not be feasible in all communities, but for people who have difficulties forming close relationships, involvement in a number of more 'superficial' relationships, where no demands are really placed on the individual, has much to recommend it.

Using voluntary resources – 'befriending'/'buddy' schemes

Some communities and some schools will have schemes that try to bring together people who have difficulties with social relationships and individual volunteers who will work to form a relationship with the individual and do activities together with the individual. The befrienders/buddies may be the same age as the individual or, more often, a little bit older. In many ways the relationship is more like an older brother/sister or mentor rather than friend but that makes it no less valuable as a source of social support. The person involved will certainly have to do more of the work to establish and maintain the relationship and will make a lot of accommodations in order to ensure that the relationship succeeds. The length of time that these relationships sustain will vary. However, as a source of social support these schemes can be invaluable. The fact that such a scheme exists on paper is no guarantee that successful outcomes will be achieved. There are certain characteristics that make such schemes more likely to deliver constructive relationships (aside from careful screening of all those who will be involved).

- *The scheme is 'managed'* – it is someone's job to run the scheme and there is adequate time and resources to do this.

- *Care is taken to match individuals* – there are mechanisms for potential volunteers and consumers to meet each other, spend time together and see if there are some natural affinities.

- *Some initial training is given* – volunteers are given the opportunity to learn something about autism so that they can understand better the challenges for the individuals with whose lives they will become involved.

- *The relationship is supported* – the volunteers meet with the scheme manager regularly and are helped to solve the problems that arise in the relationship.

- *Attention is given to the management of boundaries* – part of the support given to those involved will be about the management of boundaries: helping the volunteer to understand the limits of involvement, how not to give misleading messages (for example, in relation to the issue of boyfriend or girlfriend) and also protecting the volunteer if the person with autism starts to cross boundaries (for example, wanting to phone 20 times a day), usually described as the person with autism becoming 'obsessed'.

Schemes that do not have these characteristics are less likely to succeed in delivering effective support to people with autism. Good schemes can be found in all sorts of places, not just in places that might be deemed 'highly advantaged'. It is not really about money, it is about understanding the vital contribution that such schemes can make to those who struggle to find a place in our society. Service agencies have a tendency to prefer investing in high profile, highly professionalized and expensive activities. It is always a good question to ask: 'Who makes more of a contribution to my son or daughter's life – a bevy of caseworkers, curriculum specialists and behavior consultants, or a buddy?'

Paying people to be involved

Although we do not pay our friends for their friendship, building social support is not about having friends. Friendship is just one example of a human relationship and it is important not to be obsessed with friendship as some sort of 'gold standard'. People with autism, especially adolescents and adults, are often so isolated that any form of positive social engagement can have a significant impact. Thus we may add to the person's circle of support by increasing the number of people who are paid to be there. This can be a person who can act as a coach or teacher or just a support for a specific interest that the person with autism has (for example, a chess coach, a skating coach, a running partner). This is part of a long-term involvement in an activity, not just a temporary class. Another approach is to hire someone close in age to the individual to support the individual in community activities where the two of them can have fun together. This is very similar to the role of people in the voluntary schemes described above and it is important that a degree of life sharing is encouraged – that the person paid is expected or allowed to share her interests with the individual with autism to see if this will in turn broaden or enhance his interests and experiences. As with the voluntary schemes, attention must be paid to supporting those paid to be involved if such schemes are to deliver quality social support that has a chance of sustaining over time.

This brings us to the fairly obvious point that all good things come to an end. The relationships described above will not usually turn into lifelong friendships. When the relationship ends, for whatever reason, the person with autism will experience disappointment, sadness and anger and these feelings may drive a temporary increase in behavioral issues. Some people will argue that we should not get people involved because of this. Such logic is disastrous as it condemns many people to lead lives of loneliness and isolation forever. Rather, we should recognize that the need for social support is a lifelong issue for people with autism. As we discuss next, we can do much to help the person with autism be more effective in social settings and this may enhance her ability to 'recruit' her own social support. However, we should not count on such an outcome. We should understand social skills training as a valuable thing to do but not a substitute for much closer attention to the development of structured services and schemes that will bring more people into the lives of people with autism…and keep on doing that. Only then will we begin to make significant inroads into the social isolation of people with autism and be able to address effectively one of the needs that contributes to some people with this label behaving badly.

From the inside out – teaching social competence to people with autism

Obviously, if we can help people with autism to be more effective in social situations then it may be that they will receive more social support (as stated above, such an outcome is not guaranteed). There is a number of approaches to enhancing an individual's social competence.

Coaching to specific situations

This is where we focus on the specific social situations that arise in an individual's life where things go wrong and try to help the individual be more competent in those situations. This can be done 'live' – so, for example, we work with the individual to teach her to:

- play a specific game with another person with whom she spends time
- speak politely to customers whose tickets she is collecting at the cinema
- maintain a conversation with someone whom she meets each week after church.

Teaching will be most effective if the task is broken into small manageable steps, if lots of prompts and help are given at first and then gradually reduced and if there is a lot of encouragement and additional reinforcement for succeeding. It will help if the skills we are teaching can be summarized into simple 'rules' which can be rehearsed verbally or written down (for example, onto cue cards that the individual can be taught to use when approaching the situation in question). Although learning rules and scripts for social situations can make the individual function rather inflexibly, doing so plays to a strength in how the minds of many people with autism work and speeds the acquisition of 'good enough' competence.

The same process can be gone through in other ways. One is to start the process in more controlled situations, such as role play. The skills can be practiced away from the real situation with a 'safe' other (parent, brother or sister, paid worker) and then the 'safe' other can work with the individual to transfer the skill to the real situation. Exactly the same teaching process is gone through, but in these controlled situations it becomes easier to use powerful teaching tools like video recording and feedback, so that the individual can literally see himself. Care is needed with video feedback – if it is just used to highlight deficiencies it will not take long for the individual to reject being filmed and to refuse to watch. It needs to be used to show strengths and successes and then gradually to examine difficulties if the individual is to gain advantage from this immensely powerful learning tool.

That same point applies to a third powerful way of coaching to specific situations – use of Social Stories™. This is an approach developed by Carol Gray and readers are referred to her publications for a more detailed consideration of this very helpful approach (see Resources section). It involves a coach (teacher, parent, paid worker) helping the individual to think about and understand better some of the social situations that arise. These situations are described in words and drawn out in pictures. The thoughts and feelings of the different participants are described and drawn (with additional cues like color to represent feelings). A lesson is drawn from the story – a rule that the individual will try to follow when this situation comes up in the future. This approach tries to go beyond just the skill element of social functioning and seeks to help the individual build an understanding about other people's thoughts and feelings and how our behavior can impact those thoughts and feelings. It addresses not just the 'what' of social functioning but the 'why'. As with video it is important not to start by using Social Stories to focus just on the situations where the individual does badly. This will lead to a rejection of the whole approach. Start with it as a way of journaling social life and then move on to it as a problem-solving tool.

Of course all these approaches can be combined:

Phillip was a very articulate nine-year-old. Other children liked Phillip and would try to play with him. He would start games and then just wander off. Although other children tolerated this, Phillip did not have any friends and was getting increasingly upset about not having friends and being 'special'. It was decided as part of the plan to help Phillip that he needed to learn to see through to the finish a game that he had started with another person. Mark, a paid worker, began this process. He and Phillip went on 'anthropological expeditions' to observe how children played

(Phillip was mad about science). Mark set up games with Phillip and reminded him of the finishing rule. As Phillip got better at finishing with Mark a co-worker was introduced to start the process of generalization. A social story was written to summarize what was being learned and Phillip got a cue card with the rule written out to carry with him as a reminder. Mark then went with Phillip into his social world (school, after school program, local park) and as opportunities arose supported Phillip to follow his rule when he got involved in games with other children. His parents supported the same theme when Phillip played with his brothers and sisters or members of his extended family.

Coaching to specific situations is the most direct way of building the competence of individuals to manage effectively the situations that arise in their everyday lives. The skills taught are specific to those situations and there should be no expectation that they would necessarily generalize, either to other similar situations (conversations with other people not just those you meet after church) or to other areas of social functioning (once you have learned to be polite to customers at the cinema you will not necessarily become more chatty with the people that you meet at the gym). It is therefore tempting to consider the possibility of a more generic approach to social skills training such as social skills groups.

General social skills training

This kind of training is usually carried out in groups under the direction of a professional. The availability of such groups varies enormously from place to place. As this is a book about what families can do directly to help their son or daughter we will not consider this approach in great depth. Social skills groups can be very helpful if they are available in your area. There are two approaches to the issue. Many groups will work on a direct instruction basis – the groups are used to identify and practice specific social skills that are commonly helpful in everyday life (speaking and listening, holding conversations, being polite, stranger awareness, purchasing in stores). An alternative approach is that developed by Steven Gutstein known as the 'relationship development intervention' (RDI) (see Resources for details). This is based on a developmental model of social functioning and seeks to build more naturalistic and fluent social functioning. RDI is offered as an individual therapy and in groups. It is a very interesting approach but requires a long-term commitment and there is no reason not to combine it with more direct approaches to helping the here and now situations in which problems arise.

Building and sustaining social support is a long-term endeavor – there are no quick fixes. It is, of course, a generally 'good thing' for all people with autism. However, it has particular significance for those individuals whose behavior is cause for concern and who have fallen off the social cliff. Their social isolation can be a direct contributor to the behavioral issues and will always make that problem worse. Resolving that isolation at all levels will certainly be part of the solution and, in a few cases, will be the only solution needed.

Summary

The problem addressed

An important background contributor to behaving badly can be the individual spinning or falling out of social engagement and being effectively in social isolation. The chapter looks at how to address this issue of social isolation so that one of the driving forces behind the behavioral challenges can be addressed.

Approaches described

- rebuilding our personal engagement with the individual:
  - building tolerance for the presence of another
  - doing activities together
  - following directions
- from the outside in – bringing more people into constructive social engagement with the individual:
  - enhancing our own relationship with the individual
  - supporting natural engagements
  - developing community presence
  - using voluntary resources – 'befriending'/'buddy' schemes
  - paying people to be involved
- from the inside out – teaching social competence to people with autism:
  - coaching to specific situations
  - general social skills training.

Ideas to think more about

Write down here any ideas taken from this chapter that you think might help your child.

Chapter 12

Loss of Personal Well-being

The second major background contributor to behaving badly is a more generalized loss of personal well-being. This can involve physical health issues, mental health issues or both. It is a pervasive state, in contrast to the transient mood issues considered in Chapter 9. It means that for much of the time the individual shows some or all of the following signs:

- general discomfort or distress

- a tendency to negative emotions especially anxiety, anger

- a lack of positive emotions such as happiness, calmness

- a lack of personal satisfaction – nothing seems to really bring pleasure

- 'driven' kinds of obsessiveness – very preoccupied with doing certain things, very upset if prevented but the doing seems to bring no calmness or satisfaction

- prominent intolerances – either new ones or the return of old ones

- an increase in explosive outbursts (loss of control) often for reasons that others find hard to identify ('out of the blue')

- a recurrence of personal health vulnerabilities, such as constipation, sinus or other respiratory problems

- a change in sleep patterns – more night waking and nights without sleep

- a change in eating patterns – eating less or eating more.

This state is present for days, weeks or months at a time. It may be a 'one-off' phase that contrasts with an earlier phase in the person's life – the person is going through a difficult patch and he has not been like this before. It may be a recurring issue – the individual may experience these phases repeatedly over time. Such a down phase or loss of personal well-being is often marked by an escalation in behavioral difficulties – either the return of old behavior problems or the development of new ones. Loss of well-being reduces the individual's tolerance to demands and intrusions. It often increases more compulsive behaviors and confrontations over these. It raises the likelihood of loss of control.

This book is about the everyday life things that we can do to help people with autism resolve their issues in constructive ways; and that is what the chapter will focus on. However, it must be emphasized that these pervasive difficulties may involve diagnosable physical or mental health difficulties. When we are helping someone through a difficult phase it is vital that the individual's physicians are involved so that the appropriate diagnostic assessments and treatments can be provided for any specific condition that is identified. What we are describing in this chapter is not an alternative to these interventions but is complementary to them. It does take on additional significance in the light of Chapter 13, which considers the use of psychotropic medications. Personal well-being is such a major issue that it needs a broad-based multidisciplinary approach – what is described here is one part of that approach.

Autism and the threats to well-being
People with autism are vulnerable to loss of well-being for a number of reasons.

Primary threats
- *Relationship formation* – the central difficulty in forming and sustaining relationships puts the individual at risk in several ways. Humans are biologically designed for interdependence – for being connected with others and functioning with them. In the modern idiom we are computers designed for networking (see Chapter 11). Having difficulty in connecting to the network leaves any individual liable to social isolation and depression. It can undermine the functioning of the immune system. It will disrupt

the development of emotional regulation. Emotional understanding and self-regulation develop out of the experience of receiving comfort and calming from another. The disruption of this experience leaves the individual very vulnerable to being emotionally overwhelmed and unable to manage his own feelings. The difficulty that we define as central to our concept of autism carries with it a major threat to well-being. It deprives the individual of many of the resources required for the maintenance of positive physical and emotional functioning.

- *Thinking difficulties* – the tendency to focus on the literal and concrete and the difficulty with imagination and problem solving make it hard for the individual to develop more future-oriented thinking, to develop hopes and dreams. Hopes and dreams are a vital resource that humans draw upon to help them through difficult times. Human life is 'nasty, brutish and short' and coming to terms with that reality is not a smart thing to do. The minds of people with autism tend to make them ultra realists and deprives them of a key resource that humans depend upon to protect and sustain their well-being

- *Physical health vulnerabilities* – we know that there are a number of chronic health vulnerabilities that are associated with autism; for example, gastrointestinal difficulties including difficulties processing wheat and/or milk and seizure disorders of one sort or another. There may be others (for example, autoimmune difficulties). What is clear is that for some people autism comes with a physical health price, not just a thinking, learning or emotional price.

- *Mental health vulnerabilities* – the evidence would support the idea that there is an intrinsic vulnerability to depression for some people with autism. Whether there are intrinsic links to other mental health categories (generalized anxiety disorder, obsessive compulsive disorder and bipolar disorder) is less clear at this stage.

As well as the threats to well-being that come with the autism territory there are threats that result from the experience of making your way in the world as a person with autism.

Secondary threats

- *The lived experience* – many people with autism find this way of being difficult to the point of being overwhelming. They recognize that they are different and do not celebrate this. They are frustrated at not being able to make friends, at not understanding social situations and getting things wrong all the time and at experiencing pain and discomfort from sensory stimuli that everyone else seems untroubled by. They may turn these feelings on themselves – feeling useless, worthless and hopeless. They may turn these feelings on others, focusing their anger and hatred on those nearest to them, their parents, whom they will blame for all their woes. While the published literature is full of inspirational tales of individuals who have battled through this and come to celebrate who they are, the lived experience for many is more troubling and traumatic and a contributor to the more pervasive well-being difficulties that are the focus of this chapter.

- *Trauma* – it is a terrible reflection on 'normal' life, on the world constructed by 'neurotypicals', that people with disabilities are more vulnerable than others to the experience of physical and sexual abuse and emotional neglect. These experiences may come at the hands of dysfunctional individuals. They may come at the hands of regimes that describe themselves as therapeutic or educational. Resilience to trauma varies a lot from individual to individual but, for sure, these experiences put many people at long-term risk of emotional difficulties such as depression and post traumatic stress disorder. If an individual with autism is traumatized in these kinds of way it is certain to impact well-being in the short term and for many it will also have a longer-term impact in this area.

Given all these vulnerabilities, it is hardly surprising that loss of well-being plays a significant role in the behavioral issues for many people with autism. What perhaps is more surprising is that everyone with this label is not affected. There are clearly some individuals with autism who are resilient in the face of their challenges, and it is an urgent task for research to identify what it is that enables an individual with autism to sustain a sense of well-being. What is the difference between those who take a heavy hit and those who get by? In particular, what are the resources available to the individual that may make a difference – the kinds of support and the personal competences or characteristics that enable the individual to turn adversity into triumph? What we can be very sure about is that IQ points and speech are not the most important resources. The keys to happiness do not lie there. There is no indication that people with high-functioning autism or Asperger's syndrome experience on average greater and more sustained well-being, than those people more severely impacted in terms of IQ and verbal competence. Indeed, there is some evidence to suggest quite the opposite.

Everyday life – the little things that we can do to retrieve, promote and sustain personal well-being

Manage demand levels

When someone is in well-being difficulties, she may not be able to cope with all the tasks and activities that she is able to cope with when in a better space. It is not wise to remove all demands from everyday life, but it may be helpful to reduce them. This will require some conscious planning – looking at the demands that are made and deciding on those that we will persist with, those that we will continue to encourage but not be insistent about, and those that we will abandon for the time being. As well-being returns, we can reinstate gradually more of the demands that go to make up the person's ordinary life.

Increase access to structured, aerobic exercise

Physical fitness is a long-term buffer against stress and illness. It promotes positive well-being and can also help retrieve well-being that has been lost. Many people with autism gift us with an interest in physical activities – hiking, biking, skating, running. They usually need support to engage in these activities and some planning is required to structure these activities so that physical fitness is built up. By bringing exercise into someone's life more frequently, we can help to rebuild that overall sense of well-being. It is not for everyone – some people with this label are couch potatoes and getting into confrontations about exercise will not be helpful. But for many, physical activities are highly preferred and we often see a very different person when they are engaged in these activities.

Increase access to other forms of exercise that promote well-being

There are other forms of exercise that can make an excellent contribution to well-being. Yoga and tai chi are perhaps the most well known. It has been my experience that people with autism get very little exposure to these approaches. It would certainly be worth trying to help more individuals access these disciplines on a long-term basis. Ideally, this should be started when the person is in a good space so that it can more readily be incorporated into the routines and structure of everyday life. But even if the individual is in difficulties and has never tried these things before, it is worth considering introducing them to these approaches. Potentially they have many advantages for people with autism – a lot of the learning is visual, there is limited use of language, they take place in distraction-free environments and there is a lot of repetition and ritual. However, they do place a demand on motor and imitation skills and these can be areas of great difficulty for some people identified as autistic.

Increase access to short-term states of well-being (use more mood management)

In Chapter 9 we looked at some of the things that can turn around a temporary negative mood (ten minutes' brisk exercise, repetitive activities, music, food, laughter, massage, aroma). Although these are short-term effects it is often important to break up the day with these things when someone is in a more pervasive state of distress. It provides relief, breaks up the tendency to perseverate on and ruminate about negative things and may enable the individual to cope better with the (reduced) demands of everyday life. Again, this requires some planning to ensure that we do fit in those short walks or massage sessions, that we do use the music that impacts mood and that the Mr Bean videos are available at unstructured times.

Develop positive memory banks…and reminisce

Some individuals have a long-term tendency to dwell upon and recall all the negative things that happen in their lives. They seem to find it hard to remember the good times and positive experiences. For others, this selective attention may not be a permanent bias but a part of being in a distressed state. It is therefore a generally good idea to set about developing more external, positively focused memory banks. These may be in the form of photo albums, scrap books, videos, a website, collections of mementos. They take time to develop and care is needed over their storage. They need to be used in the context of a comfortable interaction with the person and it must be stressed that this is a commonsense suggestion, not a technique that has been validated by research.

Engineer a low demand, positive relationship into the person's support system – a role for counseling?

When you look at the network of everyday supports around many individuals with autism (see Chapter 11), it becomes apparent that most of the relationships involve some kind of 'harassment'. Parenting, teaching and job coaching all involve making demands, setting limits, trying to get the person to do things that he is not immediately minded to do. The likely absence of friends was noted in Chapter 11. Thus, when an individual is struggling with strong feelings of discomfort and distress, it can help to draw in someone who will take a more passive, listening, 'there for you' role. It will take the pressure off the primary relationships. This can be a paid person or a volunteer (again, see Chapter 11). It will involve time together on a regular basis, doing things that are comfortable and enjoyable. It is in the context of a relationship like this that those who can speak will often speak more freely about their concerns. The temptation is then to turn this into 'therapy' and, indeed, it may be someone like a school counselor who takes on this role.

A word of caution is needed about 'therapy'. Some clinicians have found that trying to engage in talk therapy can make matters worse. Trying to work through words to achieve insight and resolution backfires and instead leads the person to ruminate more on his problems so that his emotional state worsens rather than improves. What seems more helpful is to focus talk on to problem solving – looking for tips and techniques that help with situations that arise in everyday life. It is important to listen, it is important to struggle for and to demonstrate empathy, it can be important to challenge certain ways of thinking; but it is also important to keep things moving forward and not to get bogged down in a repeated rehearsal of negative thoughts and feelings.

This is a complicated issue and merits more in-depth consideration than can be provided in a book such as this. The main point here is to emphasize that the presence of a relatively non-directive relationship in the network of social supports can have a positive impact on overall well-being. It remains a challenge of course to engineer this element and, once again, it is important to stress that this point is made on the basis of clinical experience, not published research.

Consider biological interventions not involving psychotropic medication

The question of psychotropic medication will be considered in the next chapter. It is probably the most common intervention for the well-being issues presented by people identified as autistic. Many people so identified are long-term users of powerful medications and some derive clear benefit. Still, many concerns remain and there is an urgent need to find lower-risk alternatives. More detailed consideration of these alternatives can be found on the websites of the Autism Research Institute, Defeat Autism Now and the Autism Research Unit at the University of Sunderland (see Resources section for website addresses). Some people have felt better taking high doses of Vitamin B complex with magnesium. Some have reported benefit from putting Epsom salts in their baths and there is a growing interest in the use of Omega 3 fatty acids, particularly in relation to mood swings. These are alternatives to consider – there is a limited amount of research that supports their use and some more anecdotal evidence. The decision must be taken in conjunction with the individual's physicians as what appear to be low-risk interventions are unlikely to be no-risk interventions. It is important to be fully informed about risks and benefits before making any decision. However, anything that would make a contribution to well-being, however small, without the potential for damaging the individual is worthy of consideration.

A more complex intervention that is backed by some research and much anecdotal evidence, is the use of a gluten- and/or casein-free diet. This seems to make a large contribution to the well-being of some people with autism. At the time of writing it has not proved possible to find a test that predicts which people with autism respond positively to the diet, but that may change soon. What is being learned is that those who end up responding well may initially respond with a decline in their well-being and that it may take some months before the real benefits become apparent. This would argue for caution about introducing the diet when someone is already in serious difficulties. It might be better to start when he is in a reasonable space so that he is better able to cope with any discomfort that arises from the dietary change.

There are many other 'alternative' biological approaches suggested as beneficial for people with autism and the above-mentioned websites will be a helpful starting point for those keen to get more knowledgeable about these kinds of interventions.

Everyday life – the bigger picture

We have focused thus far on interventions that are woven into the fabric of the individual's everyday life. This book is about family life and the things that we can do to be supportive on an everyday basis. However, there are times when it is important to step back from the details of everyday life and consider more broadly the question of quality of life for the individual. This broader perspective becomes especially important in adult life or when considering the transition to adult life.

Many people are miserable and distressed because they are stuck in lives that bear little relation to the people that they are. They have a placement but they do not have a life. Assessment tends to focus on skills and deficits and intervention tends to focus on teaching people to do things that they cannot do, find very hard to do or have no interest in doing. People with autism are often put together with people with whom they would never in a million years choose to spend their lives (usually people with the same label). They may be stuck in places/environments in which they would never choose to be.

It can therefore be transformational to adopt a more person-centered approach to assessment, planning and service provision. Here the focus is on identifying the kind of life that would work for the individual and building the supports that will enable that life to be realized. The focus is on the individual's competences and preferences and the things that have been known to work well. The starting point is what is important from the individual's point of view. Of course, it is recognized that some people will make choices that put them at risk, so part of the process is to identify that things that will enable the person to remain safe and healthy. Person-centered planning is not about filling out a new set of forms. It is about an attitude, a state of mind that emphasizes knowing the individual and what works and what does not work for her. It is about building supports that reflect the needs of the individual not the preferences of the provider. As such it has intrinsic appeal to many families whose plea is often for others to see their son or daughter as an individual not a label, and to see their strengths not just their deficits.

Person-centered planning can be an excellent way of developing services if an individual is living in the family home. It can be a very powerful way of thinking about life away from home and is very closely linked to the kind of provision known as supported living. Supported living services enable individuals to be in their own homes with the levels and types of support that will enable them to find and lead the lives that work for them. They are not static services but services that evolve as the individual evolves.

It is a sad fact that we lack research into so many areas of vital importance. We know little about the impact of person-centered approaches and supported living services compared to more traditional approaches to service provision. However, I have been fortunate in my professional life to have been involved in some of this work and seen how, in some cases, lives can be transformed. More specifically, I have been able to see how some individuals with autism, who have presented with long-term, very serious behavioral challenges that have been resistant to all kinds of interventions, have been able to find comfort and a life that works for them and that this is accompanied by a dramatic improvement in the behavioral issues. Of course it is not a cure. It is not the answer for everyone and we still have much to learn. But it is a sharp reminder that sometimes a focus on life will lead to the kinds of changes that we will never achieve when the focus is just on behavior.

Summary

The problem addressed

This chapter looks at how loss of well-being (physical and mental health) contributes to individuals behaving in ways that others find challenging. Loss of well-being is considered an extended phase in life not just a passing mood or state, and some of the vulnerabilities to loss of well-being are analyzed. For some people loss of well-being is a recurring issue, for others it is more of a one-off. At this stage we know little about the factors that promote resilience in people with autism.

Approaches described

- doing small (and not so small) things in everyday life:
  - manage demand levels
  - increase access to structured, aerobic exercise
  - increase access to other forms of exercise that promote well-being
  - increase access to short-term states of well-being (use more mood management)
  - develop positive memory banks…and reminisce
  - engineer a low-demand, positive relationship into the person's support system – a role for counseling?
  - consider biological interventions not involving psychotropic medication
- looking at the bigger picture:
  - using person-centered assessment to develop a life that works for the individual.

Ideas to think more about

Write down here any ideas taken from this chapter that you think might help your child.

PART 4

Think Pieces

Part 4 contains two short 'think pieces'. One reviews the use of psychotropic medications for behavior. The other discusses the idea of developing an individualized 'relationship style' as well as the specific kinds of interventions that we usually consider when trying to effect changes in behavior. These chapters are intended to stimulate thought and open up discussion. They remind us that we still have a lot to learn about supporting people whose behavior is cause for concern in effective and non-toxic ways. They do not contain practical suggestions for working with behaviors.

Chapter 13

Thinking About Drugs

Many people whom we identify as autistic and who behave badly are prescribed some kind of kind of psychotropic medication. The more dangerous the behavior and the longer it goes on the more likely this is to occur. Psychotropic medications are those drugs that are intended to influence how people think, feel and behave. This chapter is not a technical analysis of these medications but a consideration of other issues that are raised by the use of these medications.

Medication types
There are a number of different types of psychotropic medications that are promoted as dealing with specific issues.

- *Anxiety reducers* – some drugs are described as reducing feelings of anxiety. These include the older class of benzodiazepine drugs such as Lorazepam and Clonazepam and other more recently marketed compounds like Buspirone.

- *Antidepressants* – these drugs are regarded as targeting serious and sustained low-mood states. Some of them also are said to reduce the anxiety or agitation that sometimes accompanies depression. Some are also said to impact obsessive-compulsive difficulties. Again there is an older class of drugs, the tricyclics, such as imipramine and clomipramine. There is a newer class of drugs, the specific serotonin reuptake inhibitors (brand names like Paxil, Prozac and Zoloft).

- *Mood stabilizers* – these are drugs that are held to reduce extreme mood swings (manic depression, now called bipolar disorder). The oldest and still probably the most effective of these is Lithium, but now many anti-seizure medications such as Depakote and Neurontin are marketed as effective for this problem.

- *Antipsychotics* – these are the drugs that can reduce the hallucinations, delusions and emotional discomforts that are part of what we mean by 'schizophrenia'. There is an older group such as Chlorpromazine, Mellaril and Haloperidol; and a newer group such as Zyprexa, Seroquel, Risperdal, Geodon and Abilify.

The science of psychotropic medications

Much of the marketing of psychotropic medications plays up the notion that they are based on a strong scientific understanding of brain chemistry and functioning. There is a theme that these drugs regulate the chemical imbalances in the brain that underlie 'anxiety', 'depression', 'bipolar disorder' and 'schizophrenia'. In particular they are said to do this by impacting specific 'neurotransmitters' – those chemicals that manage the movement of signals between nerves in the brain. There is also a theme that the newer medications are 'cleaner', less likely to have significant, negative side effects. This science speak is misleading on a number of counts.

In the first place, the origins of psychotropic medications lie entirely in chance findings. A drug being given for one thing (for example, a heart condition) is accidentally discovered to do another thing (reduce the symptoms of schizophrenia). No drug has been designed on the basis of a clear understanding of the biochemistry of any specific mental health issue because we have no clear understanding of the biochemistry of mental health. We have much speculation about the biochemistry of mental health but most of that is derived from the chance findings that certain compounds make things better. We find that a compound works, we look at some of the chemical effects it has and argue back to that telling us what the original chemical causes are. The so-called 'new drugs' have simply evolved from the older drugs, not from breakthroughs in the understanding of what we are dealing with at the level of brain and body chemistry. Our understanding of brain chemistry and its behavioral/emotional correlates is certainly improving but is still at a relatively primitive level.

There is, in fact, no model of how the brain actually works. We hold that the key to understanding mental health phenomena lies in the brain, but we do not really know how the brain works in general, let alone what its dysfunctions actually are. This is an area where science is proceeding at an accelerating place; but our moves towards an understanding of that marvel that is the human brain is more to be measured in inches than quantum leaps.

Nor should we assume automatically that the answer lies in the brain. It is still entirely possible that we are looking in the wrong place for an explanation of mental health phenomena. There is another stunning organ in the human body, the liver. The ancients certainly regarded the liver as very significant and, who knows, maybe they will turn out to be right. At the very least the rapidly emerging science of gut–brain connections and interactions argues for some caution in being entirely brain focused.

Finally, it is not certain that newer medications are necessarily cleaner than older medications. As part of the science spin on psychotropic medications, newer (more expensive) medications are promoted as having fewer side effects than older medications. Side effects are considered separately below but, suffice it to say, newer medications can have just as serious side effects as older medications and if there is a difference its size is limited. Many of these medications have not been in use long enough for us to make any clear judgment on this issue. New does not mean clean.

So when it comes to the science of psychotropic medications a healthy skepticism is in order. This does not necessarily negate the value of these medications. Irrespective of whether we understand why they work, there is no doubt that psychotropic medications can be very powerful in relieving some forms of human suffering.

The value of psychotropic medications

The science is much stronger when it comes to the effectiveness of these drugs. There is no doubt that in a significant number of cases these drugs can relieve target symptoms such as anxiety, depression, agitation, mania and troubling hallucinations. In some cases they impact symptoms that we have no other effective way of impacting (for example, mania) or they do so more quickly and for more people (for example, troubling hallucinations). In other cases, they do as well or slightly better than psychological therapies (for example, depression). What we know mostly concerns their effectiveness with adults. There is less certainty when these drugs are used for the same symptoms occurring in children. This lack of certainty is partly because there is much less research into this area of children's health, partly because there is less agreement as to whether the symptoms mean the same things in children and partly because the research findings themselves are less clear cut. The recent controversy over the use of the newer forms of antidepressants in children is a sharp reminder of this point (there is some evidence that these drugs given to children can, in a small number of cases, increase the likelihood of suicidal thoughts and perhaps suicide attempts).

The dangers of psychotropic medications

All drugs have side effects and the long list of these can be read in the accompaniment to any prescription. At the moment it is not possible to predict who will experience what side effects (this may change as our understanding of genetics unfolds). Many of the side effects are short lived and their presence is not a predictor as to whether the drug will be effective in achieving its goal. If they are too unpleasant for a child there is often an equivalent drug that may be better tolerated.

As well as the common short-term side effects, some drugs carry a risk of serious, long-term, sometimes irreversible side effects. Some drugs, particularly those used for mood stabilization, can cause liver damage. Serious concerns apply to the drugs that target the phenomena that we designate by the term 'schizophrenic' or 'psychotic' – the so-called 'antipsychotic medications'. As a class, these drugs can cause serious health problems with the specific risk varying from drug to drug. Some will create large weight gains. Diabetes is a risk posed by some, as is eye damage. Many carry a risk for irreversible damage to the movement system, such as uncontrollable tremors that seriously impact the quality of life. Death is also a risk from the rare and mysterious phenomenon of neuroleptic malignant syndrome. Again, it is not clear that the risk profile of 'new' antipsychotics is that much cleaner than the profile of the older compounds. If there is a difference its size is limited. These are the known risks that have been learned from the use of these drugs over time.

There are then what may be called 'yet to be known' risks. Many of the newer medications have not been around long enough for us to know the effects of taking these medications over very long periods of time. Most research has a relatively short time focus. The research is on adults and we know little about the effects of using these drugs with children and adolescents, when biological systems are going through complex sequences of development and change. Already there have been concerns that newer antidepressants may have dangerous and unpredicted side effects in children that are not evident in adults. This is particularly important for the case of people with autism. They are often prescribed powerful drugs and then stay on them long term (see below); and they often start on these medications when they are children.

Drugs and people with autism

People with autism can suffer from anxiety, depression, bipolar disorder and schizophrenia just like anybody else. They would seem to be at increased risk of suffering from the affective disorders such as depression. They are entitled to receive the same kinds of treatments as other people and the use of drugs is likely to be more prevalent as many people with autism might have difficulty accessing alternative, talk-based therapies. This is not the main concern.

The main concern is that psychotropic medications are often not used for clearly defined mental health issues but for behavior control. Their target is to effect a reduction in aggression, self-injury, property damage or whatever other behavior is causing concern. These behaviors are serious, they are putting the individuals and others at physical risk and also risking the breakdown of support systems (family breakdown, loss of school placement, involvement of the criminal justice system). If drugs can safely decrease the behaviors and avert breakdowns they do a great service.

However, there are concerns. We know little of the neurochemistry of behavioral difficulties, although interesting work is being done on self-injury. There is a very limited amount of research on the use of drugs for behavioral control in people with autism but there are some positive short-term findings, with Risperdal being a recent focus of interest. The most serious concerns are threefold.

1. It is relatively easy to get a person regarded as disabled on to medications and relatively difficult to get them off. If people get on psychotropic medications they are likely to stay on them, maybe for life. Given that the most commonly used drugs for behavior control are the antipsychotics there must be grave concern about the risks of long-term usage.

2. The second major risk is that many people are given more than one psychotropic medication. They are on a cocktail that includes an antipsychotic and some other 'emotional' drug (such as an

antidepressant, anti-anxiety or a mood stabilizer). We know little about the interactions of these drugs, particularly if they are being taken together over long periods of time.

3. The third concern is the willingness to prescribe these medications to younger and younger children. It is not uncommon now to meet young (five- to seven-year-old) autistic children on the kinds of cocktail described above and it seems quite likely that they will be taking that cocktail or some variant for the rest or some good proportion of their lives.

What to do

This book is about practical, everyday things that can be done by families to help their sons and daughters with autism overcome behavioral problems so that both the children and the families can experience a reasonable quality of life. In so far as we can provide effective support for families in working through these behavioral issues, we reduce the need to consider medication.

It is important to be very clear that we do not know enough to be effective enough with all behavioral issues, using the kinds of approaches outlined in this book. The field is developing, and we can do more now than we could do 30 years ago, but it is not enough. We will continue to rely on a degree of medication support for the foreseeable future. The question then becomes how we can target that support in the most effective, least risky way possible. This outcome can be made more likely if we structure carefully the consultation with the medical practitioner. Consultations are relatively brief and the practitioner is very dependent upon the information provided to her when the question is about psychotropic medication. Her own observations of the child will be limited and there are no physical exams or tests that contribute significantly to the decision. It is all about the information that the family gives to the doctor and the questions that are asked. The first approach therefore is to prepare carefully the information that we provide. It may be worth producing a short written summary of key information that summarizes the concern and the purpose of the consultation (a format is provided in Appendix 3). This should:

1. list the specific things that the family observes that are a cause for concern. It is important to be very behavioral about this – focus on behaviors *not* interpretations. Thus we might describe our child as 'pacing a lot and vocalizing loudly' rather than as 'agitated' or 'hyperactive'

2. describe any changes over time in these behaviors – has he always been like this or has it changed...if so, when?

3. describe situations where we see these things most often and situations where we see them less often

4. separately describe our own thoughts and interpretations about what is going on. It is vital to separate our opinions from our observations.

The next step is to reach agreement with the doctor about what we think is going on – to reach some kind of a 'diagnosis'. This leads into identifying the treatment options. These might include both psychotropic medications and more 'alternative' interventions such as dietary change (for example, eliminating gluten or casein or both) or food supplements (such as Omega 3 fatty acids or high doses of Vitamin B with magnesium). The risks and benefits of the relevant options can be considered and a decision will then be reached on the course of treatment to pursue. Once the treatment is decided upon, the following questions should be addressed.

1. What are the likely positive effects of the planned treatment?

2. How quickly should the effects show?

3. What are the side effects to watch for?

4. What is our goal – what changes would count as 'success'?

5. When would it be clear whether we have achieved success or not (how long should the proposed treatment be tried for)?

6. If the treatment is successful what would be the plan for discontinuing...or not?

Medical consultations tend to be short and it is unlikely that all consultations could run to this plan. By preparing information ahead of time, by presenting it to the doctor in an accessible format and by making sure that we ask relevant questions, we will make it more likely that a drug intervention will be effective and less likely that harm will occur.

Some other relevant medications

There are other medications that impact behavior and that are rather different from the psychotropics considered above. There are the stimulants such as Ritalin that are used to help focusing and learning in children and adults diagnosed with attention deficit disorder (with or without hyperactivity) and that can also improve their more general behavioral functioning. These drugs themselves are the subject of tremendous controversy because of their very widespread use and the ease with which attention deficit diagnoses are given. However, as a class of drug they have been around for a long time and their use has been researched extensively with children. Although the reasons for their effectiveness are more speculation than fact they are clearly effective in some cases and they do not appear to have highly dangerous side effects. There is no reason why someone with autism cannot also have attention deficit disorder (whether there is some overlap between the two phenomena is not clear at this stage). Their problem when used for people with autism is one of diagnosis. It can be hard to identify accurately an attention deficit in the context of autism, where attention tends to be deployed in unusual ways and where social understanding is limited so that 'following the social rules' is a challenge. Thus the research on the use of stimulants with autism has not been very encouraging and it does not take much imagination to understand that a misdiagnosis might lead to stimulants being given to someone who is highly anxious and that this would be likely to make matters a lot worse. These drugs are therefore not much used for people with autism and are certainly not indicated for behavior control in the absence of a clear-cut diagnosis of attention deficit disorder by a competent practitioner.

There are a few other medications that can be helpful and that are more driven by a theory about what is going on. Escalations in behavior are sometimes accompanied by a breakdown in the sleep system and this loss of sleep can, in time, exacerbate the behaviors of concern. Melatonin is a hormone that occurs naturally and plays a role in sleep regulation. It has been around for a long time and has been the subject of some research with people identified as autistic. It appears to aid sleep maintenance in some. Like most sleep medications it is probably best used in the short term, to help restabilize the system. Some people do use it long term and this is where there would be concerns because of the lack of research on long-term usage.

Severe self-injurious behaviors have long been a serious concern to all those involved in the lives of people with autism. Mild forms (such as hand biting) are very common but there are some people who attack themselves with such ferocity that they can do very serious damage (brain damage, loss of vision), even to the point of potentially killing themselves. Behavioral approaches have proved helpful in the short term but severe self-injury has a high risk of recurring and is generally regarded as a 'chronic condition'. There has been speculation that some self-injury is maintained because it triggers the release of internal pain killers, the endogenous opiates, and that therefore the behavior is like an addiction. There has been some evidence of abnormal activity in the opiate system of some people who self-injure severely. There are drugs that block the sites in the brain that take up the opiates and therefore prevent the 'fix' from being experienced. These drugs (naloxone and naltrexone) have proved helpful in a small number of cases of severe self-injury, although who responds and at what dose levels over what periods of time is less clear. However, given the serious and intractable nature of the problem, these successes are noteworthy.

Drugs and behavior...again

The behaviors that concern us are mainly about people with autism dealing with important issues in their lives – dealing with wants and needs, discomfort and incomprehension, change and upset. In so far as we can understand these real world issues we can learn to be helpful. We can alleviate the problems and/or help people deal with them in a way that is not costly to themselves or others. The better we understand what concerns the person with autism, the more effective we can be. We do understand a lot more now than we did 40 years ago. It must be emphasized that the issues driving behavior are mostly real world issues, the sorts of problems and dilemmas that trouble any human being. They are not driven by the caprices of internal chemistry. The idea of behaviors driven by internal chemical changes that occur quite independently of life experience probably applies to a very small subset of the behaviors that concern us. In theory we should be able to move towards a psychotropic-free world for people with autism.

In practice we can only aspire to this. The approaches described in this book all take time and a lot of hard work before results are achieved. Sometimes the pressures on families are so great that we need a quicker fix and medication can offer this. Sometimes we have no clue as to what is really going on for the person but, again, the situation is so serious that something has to be done. Perhaps also future research will identify some behaviors that do reflect internal processes that are relatively 'free running', not controlled or much influenced by life experience.

Thus psychotropic medication will be part of the spectrum of interventions for behavioral issues into the foreseeable future. It should be a diminishing part. The concern is that rather than being a diminishing part it is becoming an increasing part. The concern is that it is becoming a part at earlier and earlier ages and for longer and longer periods of time. The concern is that the scientific credibility of the drugs used is consistently overplayed. The concern is that those who suffer irreversible damage because of these medications remain uncompensated and struggle, usually as impoverished adults, to access good quality medical care. If drug companies are allowed to market aggressively the marvels of modern psychotropic medication, should they not be aggressively held accountable for injuries that are directly attributable to their products?

> Cameron is in her thirties now. She has developmental disabilities that have always impacted her quite severely. She used to be a bit of a 'wild child', throwing furniture and generally causing mayhem when she got upset. She does not do that now. She used to ride a bike and swim. She does not do that now. Indeed, she does not do very much of anything now. Her gait is unsteady, her arms move in a jerky uncoordinated way and her mouth twitches uncontrollably. She did not used to be this way. She got this way following the prescription of an antipsychotic tranquillizer for behavior control. She will stay this way now. She lives in a group home and she is poor so that her access to quality health care is limited.

As things stand right now it seems that all that we can say to Cameron is 'hard luck'. Somehow that does not feel quite right.

Chapter 14

Specific Interventions – Relationship Styles

This book has been about understanding some of the reasons why people with autism behave in ways that are challenging and then doing specific things to improve the situation. We implement plans and it is through the specifics of these plans that change occurs. However, it is very well known that reliably and persistently implementing detailed plans in real world contexts is very difficult. There is much talk of the 'implementation gap'. This is partly to do with the effort involved, partly to do with expectations and partly because the interventions may require us to do things that do not come naturally to us. This notion of what is natural takes us into a broader perspective. Perhaps there are ways of relating together, styles of relating that do a lot of the work we have been describing 'automatically', as part of the general ebb and flow of the relationship. Perhaps there is an important concept of 'fit' in relationships between people. If there is a good match between people messages will pass more easily between them, there will be better communication and understanding and problem solving will take place in a natural way. If this were true it would reduce (but not eliminate) the need for highly specific interventions.

This idea has arisen at various points in the text. The question of relationship formation, spending time on (re)building our relationship with the person, has been seen as a potential focus in a number of specific behavioral issues. We have acknowledged that there are times when people with autism become inaccessible to us, when they drift away and can no longer hear and respond to us. That then becomes the issue that we need to address before we can be effective with our specific plans. When discussing the question of 'tyranny' in Chapter 10, we discussed the need to adopt a particular set of attitudes and a certain style of relating as a context within which we negotiate limits and teach/motivate self-control.

There is also a range of research literature that consider this question of relationship style. There is a large literature on parenting in general that considers parenting style and shows that certain styles of relating might be associated with different outcomes for children, specifically in relation to internalizing social values and exercising self-control. There is a large research literature that began in the adult mental health field and has looked at the question of expressed emotion, showing that people with schizophrenia might be more vulnerable to breakdown if they are involved with people who freely express a lot of intense feelings. There is the whole literature on attachment that looks at how patterns of interaction that go on in early life are associated with later emotional and behavioral issues for children. One might even speculate that intensive early intervention using a discrete trials (Lovaas-type) approach is as much about the use of a highly intrusive, relentlessly upbeat style, as it is about the structured teaching of specific skills.

As well as the research literature, there is folk wisdom. Many people with autism who present us with major behavioral challenges do not show these challenges with some people. This goes beyond the normal observation that we tend to behave worst with those we know the best (for example, many children are worse at home than in school). It is about some people appearing to have a relationship with the individual that makes it possible for the behaviors not to occur. This is sometimes to do with specific techniques but often it is hard to pinpoint specifics – there is something about the 'chemistry' or flow of the relationship that makes things go smoothly.

It is important to be clear. In discussing relationship style we are not talking about an alternative to specific techniques. What we are talking about is the search for a powerful combination of style and technique that will bring great benefits and be more viable in real world contexts. If a good 'fit' can be achieved between two people in terms of style then it makes doing more specific things a lot easier. However, defining precisely what style is and what it does is the challenge.

There are a set of core elements that may be common to all constructive relationships. One such important element is a warmth and liking. Good fit depends on there being a liking between two people. They get on well because they like each other at some level. A second element is the creation of a listening space. Two people who fit well together are able to listen to each other, read each other's signs, take on board information from each other. This is more about willingness than cognitive capacity.

> It is not about whether I understand the words that you say but whether I think you are worth listening to, whether the information you give is credible, whether I attend closely to you in a way that I may not to others, whether your information is authoritative.

The third element of good fit is motivation. People who fit well together can inspire each other to tackle challenges, cope with difficulties. A fourth element is about balance and mutual respect.

> I am not going to bully you and make you do everything that I say but nor am I going to fall over myself to make everything all right for you and let you push me around.

As described it becomes obvious that these elements can be present in a number of influential relationships. They are present in good parents, good teachers, good therapists, good coaches.

Although it is possible to identify some of these core elements it would be a mistake to assume that there is just one way to incorporate these elements, just one perfect style. It is more about finding a way of expressing these elements that meshes with an individual's own way of being. Getting these elements into play does require adaptation to the specific individual with whom we are seeking to have an influential relationship. This is best illustrated concretely. What follows is speculative but is an attempt to describe three very different individual situations and the kind of approach that might enable one to be maximally influential.

Style 1: Nurturant/confidence building

For individuals who are sensitive or highly strung, who seem often anxious and ready to avoid situations, we will want to take a generally quiet and patient approach. We will want to show concern when the individual is stressed but will also be looking to lighten the person up, bring a smile to that face whenever we can. We will be looking for activities that we do together that are just pure fun, that give the individual a break from their acute sensitivity. We will want a lot of routine and ritual to bring security to the individual. We must be able to see possibilities for the individual and have the confidence for him that he lacks himself. That means that we are prepared to push the individual to take on challenges, to be persistent and encourage perseverance but in small ways, where success is going to be achieved. When limits are set we are going to remain firm but calmly firm, understanding that the person is emotional enough without us adding to it. In our whole approach to relating we behave in relatively low key ways – limited body language, limited emotional expression, limited speech. However, beneath the limited external expression are strong, positive feelings. There needs to be a lot of emotional engagement but it is expressed in relatively minimalist ways.

We can see this kind of style described in a number of approaches that have been generally recommended in the field – gentle teaching, options, floor time. The problem is that these approaches are described as universal approaches, in a 'one size fits all' kind of a way. What is suggested here is that they form a style that will work well with particular kinds of people or people who are at a particular stage in their lives.

This is perhaps easier to understand by offering a contrasting style.

Style 2: Assertive/authoritative (over the top and in your face)

There are people on this planet, some of whom have autism, who might be described as casual criminals, mischief makers, merry pranksters. They are underaroused extroverts who require a constant diet of strong stimulation to feel alive. They are easily bored and are not prone to outbursts of subtlety and understatement. A quiet and gentle approach with such people will pass them by.

What is needed is a much more robust and intrusive style. A lot of positive energy needs to be generated – good things require great celebrations (the big high five as opposed to the slight thumbs up). When things begin to go wrong, quickly stepping in with assertive redirection is needed, not reflective counseling and a consideration of 'What are our choices here?' When things have gone wrong, we need to mirror the 'water off a duck's back' approach – the incident is dealt with and we move on. We cannot afford to store our irritations, frustrations and resentments as these will undermine the positive energy needed to carry the person forward. While structure remains an important component of support we can afford to have greater variety and less routine and ritual with people like this and can set them bigger challenges. This is a relationship that involves strong emotional engagement but the emotion is expressed more vividly than in the nurturant/confidence-building approach.

To make clear the impact of such style issues we can imagine what happens if there is a mismatch. If a highly strung, intense individual is supported by someone who is 'over the top and in your face', it is likely that the individual will become overwhelmed, increasingly traumatized and distressed – she may become upset and disorganized around the person, refuse to cooperate at all and be very challenging. Or she may be intimidated around the particular person but the distress will show itself behaviorally around others with whom she feels more relaxed.

On the other hand, imagine a merry prankster being supported in a quiet, nurturing kind of way. It is likely that she will get increasingly out of control, as limits are not set in a way that she can take on board and not enough stimulation is provided for her to feel comfortable.

There is a third example of style, the one already described in Chapter 10.

Style 3: 'Like a rock' (the poker player's dream)

This is a style that fits with those individuals who are intensely angry, imposing rules on others in violent ways and taking more and more control to the point of being out of control. The relationship requires a degree of emotional distancing, it is a more 'professional' relationship. It is a relationship which involves commitment: commitment to stand by the individual and do all that is possible to ensure safe and positive outcomes for the individual, but engaging in a way more cerebral than emotional. It is necessary to convey strength to the individual – psychological strength not physical strength. It is a relationship in which the person supporting works to inhibit feelings of fear, anger and disappointment. Positive feelings are expressed, but in a specific kind of way – I am pleased *for* you not *with* you, you have not pleased me but I am pleased that you have shown the best side of yourself. It is a relationship that does not seek to engage in power struggles but that constantly challenges the individual to think in terms of choices and that holds him accountable for the choices he has made. While sympathy is present, pity is not. Attempts to blame others for problems are challenged. The message is – there are choices, you are a smart person, you can do this and I will help you in whatever way I can, but it is your choice. The underlying theme is that good control starts with self-control.

This relationship requires a high level of consistency from the person offering the support. It is a brutally realistic relationship – risks are readily acknowledged and clear procedures are in place for dealing with dangerous incidents. It is accepted that the individual may make such terrible choices that his future is fatally compromised but it is also recognized that there is an ever-present potential for good choices and positive outcomes.

Is life so simple?

The three styles described above are for illustrative purposes. It is not suggested that there are only three styles. What is suggested and what we have tried to illustrate is that when there is a good fit between the individual and those supporting her then a lot of important work gets done in the natural flow of the relationship and there is less need for highly specific interventions. What is also illustrated is that 'fit' is not a one time thing. People change. A style that works at one time will not be the most appropriate at another. Our approach needs to reflect the person we are with right now, not the person he once was or the person we would like him to be.

Is this feasible?

This topic raises many issues, but here we will consider two:

Can we identify the style best suited to the individual?

Three styles are described above because they serve to illustrate more generally the ideas of style and fit. We can get closer to individualizing this approach if we ask a series of questions. The first questions are about the individual.

- What kind of personality traits do we see the individual as possessing?

- What best characterizes the individual's emotional life – what feelings are evidenced, how often, with what intensity?

- What thinking style best characterizes the individual – what things tend to be the focus of attention? How well can the individual sustain attention? How easily can the person switch focus from one topic to another? How do problems or new situations tend to be tackled? What things does the person fail to notice or make sense of?

- What have we learned about supports that do and do not work with the individual? What things have we tried that have helped the individual understand, learn and feel good? What things have we tried that have definitely not worked?

The second set of questions is about the characteristics of individuals who have supported the person in the past.

- Who are the people who have been most effective in promoting comfort, understanding and learning?
- Who are the people who have been less effective?
- How do these two sets of people differ in terms of:
  - attitude
  - emotionality – emotional states and overtly expressed emotion
  - ways of communicating – amount of speaking, type of speech (level of directiveness), amount of body language, use of formal communication supports
  - assertiveness/intrusiveness
  - energy/activity level?

From these two sets of questions we can then draw up a list of (no more than ten) items that best characterize the relationship style that seems most likely to help the individual understand, learn and feel good.

Can we adapt our own personal, preferred styles to 'fit' most effectively with the individual?

This is a very crucial consideration. We are who we are, and each of us develops over time a style of conducting ourselves that reflects who we are. If our personal style is a good fit with the individual at this moment in time, that is a bonus. What if it is not a good fit, or if it was once a good fit but is no longer? Is it possible for us to change to effect a better fit? Can we as a parent or teacher or support worker change our style to effect a better fit? It sounds daunting, but that is partly because we tend to define style as some kind of inbuilt, unchangeable characteristic. There may be certain things that are unchangeable but there is plenty of evidence that many things can be changed. Again we can draw on the formal literature and folk wisdom. At the formal level we have multiple sources – assertiveness training, leadership training, training in counseling – that indicate both that specific skills and general styles can be taught to people who have not come by them naturally. At the level of folk wisdom many parents and teachers will readily point out that drama and role playing are part of what they do, that sometimes you have to put on a 'performance' to get a point across and behave in ways that are against your natural inclinations.

So there is little reason to doubt that personal styles can be changed, that we can learn to do things that differ from what comes naturally to us. The question then becomes whether it is worth investing the time and effort required to change style. Will it achieve important outcomes for the children and adults about whom we are concerned? That is the question that cannot be answered with any certainty. We will need to accumulate more folk wisdom and initiate more research to address this issue. However, it is time to look for new ways of addressing the problem that lies at the heart of this chapter – that it is often difficult to implement and sustain highly specific and 'artificial' interventions in real world contexts. This problem makes it hard for us to be as effective as we need to be in supporting those whom we identify as autistic and who trouble us with their behavior. Time and research will tell whether a focus on relationship style as well as technique will increase our effectiveness.

Chapter 15

Conclusion: Which Planet?

Autism has moved from being a small social issue to being a very large social issue. More people these days know about autism and are involved in some way. Highly articulate people with autism have begun to make their voices heard. They have been able to describe their experiences and tell their stories, but also to begin to point out that there are many positives to their way of being in the world. They have challenged the tendency of the neurotypicals to pathologize autism, to see people with autism as damaged goods rather than being people with a different view and a different set of priorities. They have reminded us that they are people who have gifts to bring rather than burdens to impose.

The voices of families have also become stronger. The families of people with autism have always been quite forceful as a group, but as the numbers have grown so too has the influence that they are able to exert. They have become a key force in both determining the services that are provided and the research that is to be done.

These burgeoning conversations and their challenge to the professional hegemony in the field is an exciting development that is already driving very positive changes in both attitudes and practice. However, I have a concern about the tendency not just to emphasize people's unique differences but to characterize people with autism as not quite human, as different in some qualitative way from 'normal' people. The idea of them being from another planet or of having some separate culture can be a playful way of reminding others to take care to recognize the unique perspective they bring to a situation. On the other hand, an historical analysis would urge great caution in making too much of this kind of characterization.

The history of social attitudes to those who are different and have difficulty meeting the requirements of a society illustrates a recurring tendency to portray them as not fully human. At various points in history, 'outsiders' have been portrayed as children of the devil, more like animals than people, perhaps some missing link in the chain of evolution. This view has been accompanied by exclusion from society and harsh and inhumane treatment. This has been fueled when the difference is seen to pose some kind of threat to society, and fear has developed that society would be damaged if those who were different were allowed to roam freely and intermingle in society. In modern times, science fiction provides a medium for portraying difference – the notion of 'aliens'. One then only has to consider how aliens are viewed in popular culture. With rare exceptions like ET, aliens are portrayed as threatening, meaning harm to the world and needing to be fought against and exterminated. It is but a small attitudinal step from the bumbling characters of *Third Rock* to the ruthless, stricken 'replicants' of *Blade Runner*.

The concern raised here is more than just the potential for harm if people with autism are portrayed as not fully human. It goes beyond liberal sentimentality. It is also a question of psychological accuracy. If we look beyond the specifics of what this book is about, if we look at the broad needs that underlie behavioral challenges and the resources people with autism need to move beyond these challenges, we see that what is being described is a very human agenda.

In summary, we have illustrated that behavioral support work is about:

- helping people forge constructive relationships and develop social support
- making the world understandable
- helping people be understood by others
- teaching people the competences needed to manage and cope with the world that they experience
- helping people experience control in their lives
- relieving discomfort and promoting well-being.

This is exactly what all human beings need. We are not addressing any kind of unique or unusual need. To be sure, some of the ways that we use to meet these needs are a little different. However, once the approaches are described (for example, putting information in visual format) it becomes obvious that everyone would benefit from them – they are not some unique form of intervention that benefits only those described as autistic. Everyone benefits from greater clarity, from structure and ritual, from thoughtful relationships, from steadfastness in those around them. There is nothing truly unique about the needs of people with autism, nothing that sets them apart from neurotypicals in a radical, qualitative way.

People with autism are not travelers from some other world. They are fellow travelers in this world, on the journey of human life. Like the rest of us, their route and their destination may be individual, reflecting each person's unique qualities and unique circumstances. Like the rest of us, they need to be able to understand what is going on and have some say in that. Like the rest of us, they need the tools and equipment that will help them on the journey. Like the rest of us, they need good company on the journey and expert guidance through difficult terrain. Like the rest of us.

Supports That Work –
What We Have Learned

The book has emphasized building our interventions for the person with autism on what we already knew about supports that work, or not, for him. A number of exercises are reproduced here to help consolidate and focus what we have learned:

- responding to behavior (Exercise 3.1 Supports that help – what we already know)

- coping with discomfort (Exercise 4.1 Management of discomfort)

- coping with difficult situations (Exercise 5.1 Contributors to success in difficult situations)

- coping with denial and limits (Exercise 7.2 Coping with denials and limits)

- mood management (Exercise 9.1 Mean…moody…? Magnificent!).

Exercise 3.1: Supports that help – what we already know

List what you know about supports – ways of working that are effective and ineffective with the person that you know.

	Supports that are generally effective/helpful	Supports that are generally ineffective/counterproductive
Ways of diffusing escalation		
Ways of responding to dangerous behavior		

Exercise 4.1: Management of discomfort

List all the things that your child finds uncomfortable, rate how intense the discomfort is and list how your child deals with the discomfort.

Things that cause discomfort	Level of discomfort usually experienced	Ways she deals with the discomfort

Review this exercise and see if it suggests any ways of working to help the person deal with the most intense situations.

Exercise 5.1 Contributors to success in difficult situations

The first step is to list the situations (transitions, unstructured times, mornings, evenings, waiting times) in which things often go badly from a behavioral point of view. Next to these, list similar situations that often go quite well – when there is less likelihood of behaviors occurring (they may occur sometimes but not often). When we compare the two lists, we may get some ideas about what makes the difference – what it is that makes those similar situations go well. This in turn may generate some ideas about how to improve the situations that are currently difficult.

Situations in which things often go badly	Similar situations in which things often go well

Ideas for changing the approach to difficult situations:

Exercise 7.2 Coping with denials and limits

List below everyday situations involving denials and limits. List the ones where the individual often copes well, the ones that often lead to a meltdown and the ones that can go either way. Review these lists and identify what it is that enables the individual to cope well in these situations.

Denials/limits often coped well with	Denials/limits that often trigger behavior	Denials/limits that can go either way

Summarize your thoughts about what factors contribute to a denial/limit being successfully coped with.

Exercise 9.1 Mean...moody...? Magnificent

Fill out the following for your child:

Signs of comfort/positive mood

Signs of discomfort/negative mood

Things that promote comfort/positive mood

Things that create discomfort/negative mood

Things that can turn discomfort/ negative mood into comfort/ positive mood

What ideas does this suggest for reducing the liklihood of the behaviour that is of concern?

Appendix 2

Learning Log

The learning log helps us to keep track of the supports that work and do not work for the person with autism in our lives based on the new things that we are trying. It tracks the problems that we solved and how we solved them. This may help us solve new problems in the future or quickly resolve a past issue that recurs. The log will also prove helpful to new people who come into the life of the individual with whom we are concerned, so that they can play a constructive role as quickly as possible. Finally, for some of the individuals themselves the log may be of value in improving self-awareness and self-esteem.

A sample log is provided on p.211. In an ideal world we would fill out the log every time we tackled an issue. Some families may manage to do this. Most will do it some of the time, perhaps when they remember or when it is a particularly important issue. Either way, the log can play a useful role. The very existence of the log is a clear reminder of how important it is to listen to the individual and learn from her the things that work and don't work, rather than having supports determined by 'experts' in autism. The real experts are the individual and those closest to her. What other 'experts' can add is icing on the cake, not the cake itself.

The log is laid out to facilitate the learning process, to enable us to pinpoint exactly what has been learned. Information is entered under a series of headings.

- *Problem addressed* – be as clear as possible in stating the problem. Try to define the problem in terms of things that are easily observable – a specific skill to increase, a specific behavior to decrease, a specific situation that we want the individual to cope with differently.

- *Things we tried* – list here all the various interventions that we tried in order to solve the problem.

- *Things that definitely worked* – list the things we tried that definitely seemed to lead to an improvement in the situation – they may not have fully resolved it but they definitely seemed to help.

- *Things that definitely did not work* – list the things we tried that definitely did not seem to lead to an improvement in the situation – they may have had no effect or they may have made the situation worse. It is important not to be too quick to judge an intervention unhelpful. All interventions take time for their effects to show. Just because something did not work the first time we tried it does not mean that it might not work if we persevered. Only enter in this column the things that we tried and persevered with but that seemed not to work.

- *What we have learned* – enter in this column a summary of what we have learned from working on this problem. This may be very specific – that certain things worked or did not work. It may be some more general proposition about what helps the person (for example, 'Bill generally does better with fewer people involved, not too much talking and having things written down').

The log itself is a diary that is continued over time. As it gets longer it gets harder for anyone new to understand quickly the most important things to know about supporting the person. Every so often it will be helpful if the family go through the log and transfer the key points to a summary sheet (log summary, p.212) that details the important things to know about supporting the individual.

Learning log

Problem addressed

Things we tried

Things that definitely worked

Things that definitely did not work

What we have learned

Log summary

List here the most important things to know about supporting our child:

1.

2.

3.

4.

5.

6.

7.

8.

9.

10.

Appendix 3

Parent–Doctor Consultation

This format is to help a family get the best out of a medical consultation on their son or daughter. It is particularly suited to an initial consultation and/or where the nature of what is going on is uncertain. It is divided into two parts. The first part helps to summarize the family's concerns and observations about these concerns. Ideally it should be provided to the doctor ahead of the actual consultation. The second part details the plan(s) to be followed to address the concern(s) and is worked out during the consultation itself. The format allows for a consultation to address several concerns, although the more specific the focus of a consultation, the more likely it is that a clear and relevant plan will emerge.

Consultation focus

TO: Dr.

FROM:

CLIENT:

DATE:

	Concern 1	Concern 2	Concern 3
Describe what is going on that causes concern.			
How long has this been going on? When did it start?			
Is it getting better, worse or staying much the same?			

Consultation focus continued

	Concern 1	Concern 2	Concern 3
Describe any situations in which it occurs a lot / seems much worse?			
Describe any situations in which it rarely occurs / seems much better?			
What has been tried already to deal with this concern?			
Describe the changes you are hoping to achieve.			

Consultation plan

	Concern 1	Concern 2	Concern 3
Diagnosis – what the concern is thought to mean.			
Further assessments to be undertaken.			
Suggested treatment.			
Likely positive effects of suggested treatment.			

Consultation plan continued

	Concern 1	Concern 2	Concern 3
Possible negative effects – describe.			
How long should treatment be continued before deciding if it is helpful or not?			
If the treatment is helpful can it be discontinued?			
Alternative treatments that can be considered for this diagnosis.			

Resources

This is a 'personal' book, deliberately written without references in the text itself. It comes out of 30 or more years of practice, reading and research. None of the ideas are original and below are listed some of the resources that guide my current thinking and have been drawn on for this book.

Print resources

American Psychologist (2000) January. Special issue on happiness, excellence and optimal human functioning.

Carr, E.G., Horner, R.H., Turnbull, A.P. and colleagues (1999) *Positive Behavior Support for People with Developmental Disabilities. A Research Synthesis.* Washington, DC: AAMR.

Clements, J. with Martin, N. (2002) *Assessing Behaviors Regarded as Problematic for People with Developmental Disabilities.* London: Jessica Kingsley Publishers.

Clements, J. and Zarkowska, E. (2000) *Behavioural Concerns and Autistic Spectrum Disorders: Explanations and Strategies for Change.* London: Jessica Kingsley Publishers.

Delaney, R. and Kunstal, F.R. (1997) *Troubled Transplants. Unconventional Strategies for Helping Disturbed Foster and Adopted Children.* Oklahoma: Woods 'N Barnes Press.

Field, T. (2000) *Touch Therapy.* London: Churchill Livingstone.

Fouse, B. and Wheeler, M. (1997) *A Treasure Chest of Behavioral Strategies for Individuals with Autism.* Arlington, TX: Future Horizons.

Frith, U. (2004) 'Confusions and controversies about Asperger syndrome.' *Journal of Child Psychology and Psychiatry, 45,* 4, 672–86.

Gutstein, S. (2000) *Autism Aspergers: Solving the Relationship Puzzle.* Arlington, TX: Future Horizons.

Gray, C. and White, A.L. (2002) *My Social Stories Book.* London: Jessica Kingsley Publishers

Harvard Mental Health Letter (2002) 'The novel antipsychotic drugs.' 19, 3, 1–3.

Journal of Child Psychology and Psychiatry (2002) Special section on social cognition. 43, 7, 847–916.

Keltner, D., Gruenfeld, D.H. and Anderson, C. (2003) 'Power, approach and inhibition.' *Psychological Review, 110,* 2, 265–284.

Levy, T. and Orlans, M. (1998) *Attachment, Trauma and Healing.* Washington, DC: CWLA Press.

Lucyshyn, J.M., Dunlap, G. and Albin, R.W. (eds) (2002) *Families and Positive Behavior Support: Addressing Problem Behavior in Family Contexts.* Baltimore, MD: Paul H. Brookes.

Miller, W.R. and Rollnick, S. (2002) *Motivational Interviewing. Preparing People for Change.* New York: Guilford.

O'Neill, R.E., Horner, R.H., Albin, R.W., Sprague, J.R., Storey, K. and Newton, J.S. (1997) *Functional Assessment and Program Development for Problem Behavior. A Practical Handbook.* Baltimore, MD: Paul H. Brookes/Cole.

Ozonoff, S., Dawson, G. and McPartland, J. (2002) *A Parent's Guide to Asperger Syndrome and High-Functioning Autism.* New York: Guilford.
Richer, J. and Coates, S. (eds) (2001) *Autism – The Search for Coherence.* London: Jessica Kingsley Publishers.
Schopler, E. (ed.) (1995) *Parent Survival Manual.* New York: Plenum Press.
Schroeder, S.R., Oster-Granite, M.L. and Thompson, T. (eds) (2002) *Self-Injurious Behavior: Gene–brain–behavior Relationships.* Washington, DC: American Psychological Association.
Thayer, R.E. (1996) *The Origin of Everyday Moods.* Oxford: Oxford University Press.
Valenstein, E.S. (1998) *Blaming The Brain.* New York: The Free Press.
Volkmar, F.R., Lord, C., Bailey, A., Schulz, R.T. and Klin, A. (2004) 'Autism and pervasive developmental disorders.' *Journal of Child Psychology and Psychiatry,* 45, 1, 135–70.
Willey, L.H. (2003) *Asperger Syndrome in Adolescence.* London: Jessica Kingsley Publishers.

A very important influence is the growing literature written by people with autism themselves. I have not read all the books available but have been inspired by what I know of the works of Temple Grandin, Luke Jackson, Wendy Lawson, Liane Holliday Willey, Donna Williams and Dawn Prince Hughes.

Web resources
Families for Early Autism Treatment provide a valuable daily newsletter covering recent research, social policy issues and human interest stories: *www.feat.org.*

There is a lot of interest in biomedical interventions for people with autism, with The Autism Research Institute and Defeat Autism Now playing a leading role in promoting and disseminating current thinking (*www.autism.com/ari/*), as does the Autism Research Unit at the University of Sunderland, UK (*http:/osiris.sunderland.ac.uk/autism/*).

The movement to person-centered perspectives in learning how to support people has been very influential for me, in particular the work of Michael Smull. Much useful information and materials can be found at *www.allenshea.com.*

Autism is a heavily professionalized field but much of the most crucial help a family gets will come from other families. This point is brilliantly illustrated by Parents Helping Parents, Santa Clara: *www.php.org.*

The behavioral field has been transformed by the shift to positive behavior support, represented by the Association for Positive Behavior Support: *www.apbs.org.*

Index

abuse *see* trauma
adolescence 137, 138, 150, 162
adulthood 112, 113, 150, 162, 176, 190
    transition to 150, 156–7
    see also adolescence
agitation 129
    signs of 84
    see also diffusing agitation; escalation of
        agitation; mood, management
analysis *see* risk-benefit analysis
anger 122, 132, 138, 151, 195
    coping with 98, 103, 127, 195
    increases in 17
    related to loss of personal well-being 17,
        168, 171
    related to loss of social connectedness
        162
anxiety
    caused by disruption to routine 30
    in families 139
    loss of personal well-being 17, 119, 168
    over-stimulation 14
    reducing 55, 87, 91, 193
        medication 181, 183, 185–6
    see also mental health
aromatherapy 37, 54, 56, 75, 76, 126, 134, 173
assertiveness, importance 37, 90, 122, 194, 197,
assessment 176
attachment 156, 192
    see also relationship(s); social, engagement
attention
    focusing 64, 65, 73–4, 130, 196
    shifting 64, 65, 67–9, 91–2, 103, 105,
        106, 129, 196
    see also distraction, as an approach to
        behavior
attitudes
    of support person 197
    social 200

auditory integration therapy 61
aversives 35, 114
    see also behavior, reducing by, response
        cost

behavior 9
    assessment of 29, 86
    as communication 14–15, 77, 82–3
    costs of 9–11, 12, 52, 109–10, 112
    momentum 92
    physically incompatible 54, 115
    plans, implementing 18, 191, 198
    reducing by
        extinction 32, 44, 88–9, 111, 116
        response cost 31, 34–5, 145
        reward 59–60, 79, 114–16
        teaching alternative skills 31, 33, 55–6,
            77, 89–90, 112, 116
    responding to 11, 29, 30–45, 105, 203,
        204
    sequencing 159
    types of 10
biorhythms 64, 75, 120, 129
bipolar disorder 124, 170, 182, 183, 185
    see also depression; mental health
boredom 14, 74, 194
buddy schemes 161–2
bullying 27, 122

calming 37, 84, 124, 131
    see also mood management; self-calming;
        self-control/ regulation
choice
    about behavior 33, 34, 104, 146, 156
    asserting the right to 91, 195
    difficulties with 64, 113–4
    explaining/offering 67, 69, 103–4,
        156–7, 176
    making 105–6
cognition *see* thinking
communication 197
    teaching as alternative to behavior 56–7,
        85–90, 116
    see also behavior, as communication; visual
        communication